Challenging the Colonialism in World Language-Learner Literature:

Paths for Writing Toward Respectful Interculturality

****

written for world language teacher colleagues
who are not members of the cultures
that speak the language that they teach, and
who want to create language-learner literature
while respecting cultures
and honoring movements for #OwnVoices

Ideas authored by the "STAYING IN OUR LANES PROJECT" Team
Book written by Kristi Lentz with Adriana Ramírez and Cécile Lainé

Spring 2021

Cover Art by Santiago Aguirre

Copyright © 2021
Kristi Lentz with Adriana Ramírez and Cécile Lainé

All rights reserved. No part of this publication may be reproduced, stored in a retrieval system or transmitted in any form or by any means – electronic, mechanical, photocopying, and recording or otherwise – without prior written permission of the author, except for brief passages quoted by a reviewer in a newspaper or magazine. To perform any of the above is an infringement of copyright law.
ISBN: 978-1-7371073-0-9

TABLE OF CONTENTS

FOREWORD... 4
Dr. Cécile Accilien and Dr. Krishauna Hines-Gaither

OPENING..7

- Preface.........7
- Introduction.........8
- About the "Staying in Our Lanes Project" 11

PART I: OBSERVATION……………………………………………………...15

PART II: ANALYSIS

1. Analyzing the Problem(s) …………………………………………………...20

2. Identifying Philosophical Frameworks …………………………………...27

- Framework 1: Navigating Sociopolitical Categories……….27
- Framework 2: Acquisition of Respectful Interculturality………28
- Framework 3: "Staying in Our Lanes": A Metaphor………..29
- Framework 4: Stories that "Belong" to Others + The Problems We Perpetuate………31
- Framework 5: Studies of Global Colonialism and Critical Theory………36
- Framework 6: Windows, Sliding-Glass Doors, Mirrors and Curtains………37
- Framework 7: #OwnVoices………38
- Framework 8: Cultural Styles of Storytelling………..40
- Framework 9: Moving Beyond Binary Paradigms………41

3. Defining Terms and Concepts…………………………………………………..43

PART III: ACTION

4. Engaging with Cultural Consultants & Sensitivity Readers………………….53

5. Writing Along the Paths

  * Paths Overview Chart…………………………………………………………..56

  * Path A: Authoring Stories from Your Own (Sub)Cultures……………………..58

* Path B: Collaborating..63

- Model B-1: Paired thematic stories.........63
- Model B-2: Interwoven voices in a single book.........65
- Model B-3: Cowriting.........67
- Model B-4: Adaptation.........68
- Model B-5: Graphic Novel Co-Production.........70

* Path C: Facilitating...72

- Model C-1: Ghostwriting.........72
- Model C-2: Recruit a New Author & Serve as Consultant.........74

* Path D: Scribing (Language Experience Approach / Dictated Stories)...........76

6. Responding to Q & A..81

7. Summarizing: Traffic Light Graphic..84

8. An Invitation to Continual Innovation, Transparency & Accountability............85

9. Post-Note..86

AFTERWORD

10. Appendices..87

- Appendix I: Sensitivity Notes on Path D (Scribing).........86
- Appendix II: FAQs on the #OwnVoices Movement.........89
- Appendix III: Recommended Resources.........91

11. Works Cited...95

12. About the Authors..101

FOREWORD

by Dr. Cécile Accilien and Dr. Krishauna Hines-Gaither

This work could not come at a better time. We are in a period whereby several institutions and individuals are creating space to have complex and meaningful dialogues about inclusion, power, privilege, positionality and cultural appropriation. As language instructors, we are intertwined and intimately linked with the cultures that we represent in our classrooms. As such, we have a responsibility to start with our own uncolonization, our own unconscious bias and deep reflection of the ways in which we interact with other cultures. Our personal introspection will create spaces for our students to learn the importance of uncolonizing their own minds as global citizens. The authors push us to think about complex questions such as: Who has the right to appropriate a certain culture and make a profit (whether academic or financial)? How do we work with other cultures in a mutually beneficial manner as opposed to a rapport of superiority/inferiority?

This book challenges us to be mindful of our privilege, power and positionality. We must ask why we are writing, for whom, in what context and ultimately what is our true motivation? As language and cultural instructors, we appreciate the authors' invitation for us to be mindful of issues of representation, social justice, diversity, equity and inclusion. These considerations inform how we select texts for our students, and also how we write to contribute to the corpus of the language and culture in which we teach.

As scholars, teachers, students, administrators, community members and humans, we must do the work of social justice and anti-racism together. This pursuit must be constant. To become anti-racist, we have to continuously work to uncolonize our minds, thoughts, and actions. The work of social justice and anti-racism is important and necessary, especially those of us who are members of the academe. It is our responsibility to assist our students to view the world through an intersectional lens in terms of race, class, gender, sexuality, ability, religion, culture, immigration and more.

In order to have an equitable society we must acknowledge the need to uncolonize our communities through consistent action. Uncolonization and anti-racism are lifelong endeavors that necessitate openness to learning about other cultures with humility. We do not live in a post-colonial society. We live in a world that bears the enduring legacies of colonialism. Ongoing racism, sexism and microaggressions are a direct result of past and present colonial practices. We must work together to uncolonize our spaces, and to create a more socially just society within the resources and sphere of influence that we have.

Scholar bell hooks reminds us that as instructors we must "teach to transgress" because "the classroom remains the most radical space of possibility in academia" (1994, p. 12). The notion of "teaching to transgress" will be different for each of us depending upon our privilege, power, positionality as well as who and where we are teaching. However, teaching to transgress means teaching from the lens of intersectionality with a willingness to work on our own biases and prejudices. We must be willing to be vulnerable and to learn with and from our students. When we are open to co-creation, we can collectively learn to interrogate together, to challenge, to unlearn and to combat oppression. This examination will preclude us from transferring our biases on to our students.

Ann Diller wrote, "It takes considerable courage, self-knowledge, a brave heart, and honest openness to face one's own ignorance and stay present to the concomitant experiences of discomfort, perhaps feeling horrified as well as torpified" (1998, p. 8). As language and culture instructors and practitioners, we believe that this book is an essential offering to the world language community to step away from its comfort zone by incorporating anti-racist practices. This book also helps us not only to connect to other literary works, but also to produce literature that will endure the test of time. The authors of *Challenging the Colonialism in World Language-Learner Literature: Paths for Writing Toward Respectful Interculturality* offer us tangible tools to begin the essential work of introspection, positive change, and anti-racism.

Cécile Accilien, Kennesaw State University
Krishauna Hines-Gaither, Guilford College

PREFACE

In the current historical moment, many authors and publishers face the challenges of how to create books with authentic representation of literary characters from different identities. The January 2020 publication of the novel *American Dirt* brought the #OwnVoices movement to the fore, sparking a public discussion which resonates through the world language education community.

**Many world language teachers and writers
who are not members of target cultures are now asking,**

"If I honor the #OwnVoices movement in creating language-learner literature, where is the space for my own voice?"

and "Does this mean I have to stop writing?"

**We are noticing a collective sense of anxiety in our profession
as a paradigm shift is occurring in literature and culture,
and some are expressing uncertainty about the way forward.**

* * *

In response, the Staying in Our Lanes Project believes:

**- Every voice is essential.
- We all have a place from which to write.
- We can do better on how we make space for all voices.**

In our materials, we articulate models for writing that make space for everyone's voice and address the urgent need for a more respectful interculturality in language-learner literature and curricula.

Situated in the field of world language education, the Staying in Our Lanes Project seeks to nurture hope for deepened intercultural relationships in an emerging postcolonial global paradigm through the proliferation of language-learner literature. The Staying in Our Lanes Project proposes models for authors and teachers who are not members of target cultures to uncolonize our practices and increase the development of respectful interculturality by "staying in our lanes"-- refraining from authoring the stories that are not ours to write.

INTRODUCTION

This is a book of solutions.

By nature, solutions must be in response to a problem. Consequently, the first part of this book observes the problem; the second part analyzes and reflects on the problem; the third part proposes actionable paths toward transforming the problem into new opportunities.

These paths are not necessarily "new" but they are ones yet to be trod widely within the world of language-learner literature. They are seeds for thought, a beginning. Many more options within these paths will likely exist.

Parts of this work are doubling as a Master's thesis, so it reads academically, complete with footnotes. We trust that many readers will be interested in this depth and richness.

The work is principally addressed to teachers and authors with identities situated in whiteness in the U.S. and Canada. (By "whiteness," we refer to the social construct of imperial power that benefits from the systemic oppression of others. It is centered in biological whiteness but it is not limited to the biological.) <u>We are two White writers and one BIPOC writer, calling in people of whiteness</u>, asking them to freely take space in their own storytelling lanes and to get out of the storytelling lanes of others. To cease and desist from filtering the stories of historically oppressed communities through lenses of whiteness. To instead uplift and amplify for students the authentic storytelling voices of people from the communities that speak the languages we teach.

All three of us are language teachers striving to bring quality intercultural language-learning materials to our students. Two of us--Cécile and Adriana--are fiction authors within the language teaching milieu. When you read specific directions to authors, assume these are the primary voices. Two of us--Adriana and Kristi--each have studied imperialism in the Western hemisphere; for Adriana, through studies birthed of extensive readings and lived experience under imperialism in Colombia; for Kristi, through graduate studies in interculturality. When you read analyses of imperialism in Latin America, assume these are the primary voices, and when reading a discussion of challenging global colonialism, assume that Adriana's voice has the leadership. Cécile has expanded the analysis to include the Francophone world in Africa and the Caribbean, as well as has another Cécile--Cécile Accilien, a Francophone professor of language and literature, who has assisted us in preparing this book. All of us are consciously striving to dismantle systemic racism and to uncolonize our teaching, our lives and our work. The work is a fusion of our many discussions, synthesized by Kristi who physically wrote the work. It represents the voices, thoughts and co-writing of all of us, in conversation with broader discussions in our profession, in literature, in our world.

As two of the three of us are Spanish-language teachers, and Spanish is the most commonly-taught language other than English in U.S. schools, the work has a Spanish-language and Latin America-centric tone, as well as a U.S. tone. However, the principles are very applicable to teachers and writers of language-learner material in other commonly-taught world languages. The exception to applicability may be Indigenous language revitalization programs, as this work is intended for authors who are not members of the cultures that speak the target language in which they write language-learner literature, and we are assuming that creators of Indigenous language materials are cultural insiders to their languages.

In this work, we address challenging colonialism in a global sense, within our context as teachers of world language. This is intended to complement the urgent need for all of us to participate in local challenging of colonialism. We do not yet live in a postcolonial world, although hope for that paradigm is emerging through the work of many movements worldwide. When talking about challenging colonialism, we use the term "uncolonize" to describe the work that non-Indigenous peoples do to challenge mindsets and actions that perpetuate colonialism, globally and locally. For further discussion, please see "Defining Terms and Concepts" in this book.

Our Beta Audience

We are extremely grateful to the beta readers who have taken the time to read this work and offer critical feedback, as well as the participants in our Summer 2020 webinars who also served as a beta audience.

Our beta audience has been from a variety of backgrounds: seasoned writers, aspiring writers, non-writers, from a variety of racial, ethnic, gender and professional identities.

Thank you to our beta audience for showing up to listen with an open heart and for showing us that a majority response to this work is, after perhaps an initial trepidation, one of open curiosity, positivity, and inspiration to write even more than before.

We are especially thankful to Dr. Cécile Accilien, professor of language and literature with a specialization in African and African American Studies, Haitian Studies, and Latin American and Caribbean Studies, who has thoroughly examined this work as a professional consultant and critical reader. We are also deeply grateful to Dr. Krishauna Hines-Gaither for co-writing the foreword with Dr. Accilien.

A few words before we get started:

1. Our aim is to uplift. Any mention of specific texts is positive.

2. We operate on a spectrum of more-helpful to less-helpful, rejecting a binary of good-bad.

3. We're all in a process of "now that we know better, we can do better."

4. We invite readers to lean into any discomfort with curiosity.

———

ABOUT THE "STAYING IN OUR LANES PROJECT"

The "Staying in Our Lanes Project" began in April 2020. We have, so far, produced the webinar "Paths for Writing Toward the Acquisition of Respectful Interculturality" and this book.

1. WHAT WE'RE ABOUT:

Locating our work within a fusion of the concepts of "make space, take space" and "staying in our lanes," <u>we propose several paths--or *lanes*, if you will--by which writers and teachers who are not members of target cultures may create language-learner literature for not only language acquisition but also the acquisition of respectful interculturality within an emerging postcolonial global paradigm.</u> These paths respond to the poignant need, widely expressed within world language teacher networks, for avenues for creative authorship while honoring the principles of #OwnVoices--a movement in which members of marginalized[1] cultures decide how, when, why, whether and to whom to tell the stories that pertain to their culture.

We echo the words of Krishauna Hines-Gaither with regard to anti-racist work in world language education: "Our goal is to interrogate our discipline; not to tear it down, but to build it up. As language educators, we have a profound opportunity to ameliorate the way that we do business."[2] We are suggesting opportunities to change the way we create language-learner literature in order to have a more respectful interculturality.

"Interculturality," a central theme in our work, refers to "the existence and equitable interaction of diverse cultures and the possibility of generating shared cultural expressions through dialogue and mutual respect," as defined by the United Nations Educational, Scientific and Cultural Organization (UNESCO).[3] This respect and collaboration is a core piece of this work.

2. WHO WE ARE:

We are presently a collaboration of three world language teachers who love our profession and want to encourage us toward an even closer realization of our profession's goals of interculturality through language and literacy. We are working personally along the paths proposed in this book. We are:

* **Kristi Lentz** (she/her): Spanish / English teacher, non-fiction writer, and graduate student in intercultural studies; from unceded Coast Salish and Snohomish territories in

---

[1] With regard to the word "marginalized" in this book, we are using language from the originator of the #OwnVoices hashtag, Corinne Duyvis (see Appendix 3). We do not mean to put any of us in a box by referring to "marginalized" aspects of identity, for those of us with so-called "marginalized" identities may, in fact, feel empowered by virtue of those same identities.

[2] Krishauna Hines-Gaither, "Anti-Racism in the World Language Classroom," *WorldView: A Language Blog*, Concordia Language Villages, 14 July 2020, http://www.concordialanguagevillages.org/blog (Accessed 15 July 2020).
/villages/anti-racism-in-the-world-language-classroom#.Xw8PmC3Mw6V (Accessed 15 July 2020).

[3] United Nations Educational, Scientific and Cultural Organization (UNESCO), "Interculturality," Accessed September 15, 2020, https://en.unesco.org/creativity/interculturality

Snohomish County, Washington State, USA; living in unceded Northern Pomo territories in Mendocino County, California, USA.

* **Adriana Ramírez** (she/her/ella): Spanish teacher and fiction writer; from Medellín, Colombia; living in the shared, unceded traditional territory of the Katzie, Semiahmoo, Kwantlen and Coast Salish Peoples, in British Columbia, Canada.

* **Cécile Lainé** (she/her): French teacher and writer of fiction and non-fiction; from Paris, France; living in Tennessee, USA, in unceded ᏣᎳᎫᏪᏘᏱ Tsalaguwetiyi territory (Cherokee, East).

For more information on the team, see "About the Authors" at the end of this book.

How did the team form? We three were part of a larger professional cohort that formed in early 2020 to collaborate on another project. The Staying in Our Lanes Project emerged in April 2020 when Kristi and Adriana started talking about imperialism and colonization; simultaneously, Kristi had ideas percolating about possible new approaches to #OwnVoices concerns that she was hearing widely-expressed from novelists. Not being a fiction author herself, she asked Adriana, then Cécile--who *are* fiction authors--if they thought the ideas would be helpful to develop. Adriana and Cécile were enthusiastic to build on these and to make something that we could present to our larger community. We are now sharing this with our world language profession in hopes that authors of language-learner literature might experiment with these models, promote them, and innovate additional models that support movements dismantling colonization and uplifting #OwnVoices.

3. INTENDED AUDIENCE

a. Professional Identity: People working in the field of world language education: authors, consultants, teachers and literacy/language promoters.

b. Sociopolitical Identity: The original intent of this project was to propose potential solutions to authors of whiteness situated in a locus of global power--such as the U.S. and Canada--who are wondering, "Where is there space for my writing voice if I am yielding space to #OwnVoices authors from the cultures that speak the language I teach?" We addressed teachers of whiteness because dynamics of privilege and oppression have led to a disproportionate amount of White teachers in these nations of global power, and have shaped the colonizing practices that occur within the education profession--such as the deeply problematic practice of telling other peoples' stories. As such, many of the comments may be most applicable to White educators.

On further reflection, however, the struggle to honor #OwnVoices in the creation of language-learner literature likely applies to teachers and authors of *all* racialized and ethnic identities, worldwide, who identify as members of loci of global/imperial power, as few in these loci are entirely free from some degree of collusion in practices of colonization. (By "locus" and its plural, "loci," we mean "the effective or perceived location of something abstract"[4]--like global power.)

A note: Members of *regions* that have been historically oppressed by global colonial and imperial powers are not the primary intended audience. However, the project may be of strong interest to world language teachers and authors in these regions, as it proposes models for equity, justice and honoring #OwnVoices which may empower teachers and authors to resist colonizing practices from outsiders and to insist on the primacy of their own voices. It also proposes models for writing about people from other cultures (within or outside of one's own region), which authors from colonized regions may find useful. That said, however, we are not directly addressing issues of race, class and power *within* countries of Africa, Latin America and the Caribbean, and other historically-colonized countries. While that may be an important investigation, and many readers have asked us about it, it's not our place to do that work; we leave that to teams of people from within those regions to undertake that work in their context.

4. STRUCTURE OF THIS WORK: This work follows the observe-analyze-act cycle of social action/*praxis,* which is common in liberative practice. This cycle begins with on-the-ground **observation**, moves to reflective and theoretical **analysis**, and then to a plan for practical **action**. Definitions of terms have been placed prior to the action section so as to draw readers straight into the content of observation and analysis.

This book is not for profit. 100% of proceeds will go toward the group We Need Diverse Books.

Engage with the "Staying in Our Lanes Project" online:
#stayinginourlanes #stayinginourlanesproject / stayinginourlanes@gmail.com
facebook.com/stayinginourlanes / @stayinginourlanes (Instagram) / @stayingourlanes (Twitter)

Copyright 2021 by Staying in Our Lanes Project

Please contact stayinginourlanes@gmail.com for permission to reproduce this work in whole or in part. Attribute quotations to Staying in Our Lanes Project and direct readers to our social media pages.

Disclaimers: We are people in process, doing as well as we can until we know better.

---

[4] Oxford Dictionary, "Locus," https://www.lexico.com/en/definition/locus (Accessed 28 November 2020).

PART ONE: OBSERVATIONS

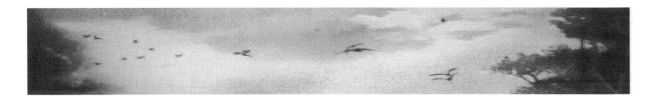

OBSERVATION: the first stage of the observe-analyze-act cycle of social action/*praxis*.

In 2020, three U.S.-based groups of screenwriters--Latinx, Black and Indigenous/Native--submitted open letters to their industry demanding greater #OwnVoices representation in screen media. We invite readers to consider how these letters might reflect concerns from a global-based context as well. (We offer excerpts due to space constraints, and strongly urge readers to access the originals at the links provided in the footnotes.)

.....

Excerpts: Open Letter from Latinx Screenwriters, October 2020[5]

"We are tired of Latinx projects being developed with no Latinx writer, director, or producer attached. We refuse to be filtered through a White perspective."

"We are tired of stories that are only about our trauma."

"No stories about us without us. Make room for us to tell our own stories."

"It is not enough to hire one Latinx writer and expect them to be the sole representative of a vast and heterogeneous group of people. Hire more of us. Listen to us. Put us in positions of power."

"We write stories of joy, origin stories, genre stories, children's stories, and much more. We demand to be seen and heard in our entirety."

"We are able to write more than identity stories. In fact, our stories are also American stories, stories of resilience, of liberation, of hope."

"We will continue to demand an industry that sees us, hears us, and values our contributions so that the world will do the same through the stories we tell."

---

[5] Untitled Latinx Project, "Open Letter to Hollywood," October 2020, https://untitledlatinxproject.com/la-letter (Accessed 28 November 2020).

"Stories are powerful. Stories change the world. Let's get on the right side of history so we can continue to create needed change and tell captivating stories together."

....

Excerpts: Open Letter from Black Screenwriters, June 2020[6]

"Black people have endured generations of systemic oppression…You were there the entire time, denying us equal representation on your sets and in your studios while perpetuating dehumanizing stereotypes about us in movies and mis-telling our stories to the world. As Black Americans, we cannot afford to deny how these racist histories have served to mischaracterize us as people, marked our experiences, and impacted how we are perceived and represented at work and around the world."

"As potential employers, you will refuse to hire us based on the assumption that we can't help tell 'mainstream' stories, and at the same time, hire a white writer to tell a narrative about Black people."

"Black writers have been critically underrepresented in this industry at the expense of consistently authentic and diverse storytelling."

"When companies and studios claim to champion diversity but refuse to prioritize hiring Black writers for a writers' room or to contribute to Black narratives, you are perpetuating a system that either exploits or excludes Black experience and perspective. Not only are you discounting the impact of Black voices to authenticate the narrative you're putting into the world, but you're telling us, your peers, that our input is not important or valuable to the work this industry produces."

"[W]e joined this industry because of our passion to connect with others by sharing our narratives, perspectives, and experiences. Now, we want white [media power] to play an active role in creating new industry systems that connect us to the access, opportunities, and compensation we have worked hard for and deserve so that we can feel secure enough to continue to help push this industry forward."

"We… are willing to do our part to continue to bring diverse, dynamic, and authentic storytelling to the rest of the world. When you need us (and you will need us), you now know where to find us."

…..

---

[6] Committee of Black Writers of the Writer's Guild of America West (WGAW), "Letter to Hollywood From WGAW Committee of Black Writers," 12 June 2020, https://www.wga.org/uploadedfiles/the-guild/inclusion-and-equity/dear_hollywood_june_12_2020.pdf (Accessed 28 November 2020).

Excerpts: Open Letter from Indigenous / Native Screenwriters, October 2020[7]

"We continue to see Native and Indigenous stories told by non-native writers who perpetuate inaccurate and racist representations."

"We challenge the film and television industry to commit to advancing Native and Indigenous representation, and actively support our qualified and emerging ... writers who hold fresh perspectives, culturally rich and varying life experiences, and talent for authentic storytelling."

"These [industry] stories — written by white men, directed by white men, and starring white men in red face — reinforced [historical myths] despite the fact that these are our homelands that we have thrived in for time immemorial."

"By failing to tell contemporary and multi-dimensional Native stories, misconceptions continue regarding the legal rights of Native Nations and contributes to the harm of Native and Indigenous women."

"Native American and Indigenous people are alive, diverse, vibrant and culturally specific. We are the lead characters of our stories and we live right now in cities, on reservations, in suburbs, and in all walks of life. ... We have a lot to offer narratives across all genres and we want to work alongside you to add our valuable, untapped perspectives and authenticity to your stories as well."

"We are not in the business of legitimizing scripts for free, or authorizing our stories for others to tell. We have seen this for more than a century, and it has only perpetuated racism toward our community by way of erasure and harmful stereotypes."

"We need you to zealously push for scripts written by Indigenous writers, TV shows run by Indigenous show-runners, filmed by Indigenous directors and portrayed by Indigenous actors to ensure we have the primary opportunity to portray our communities."

"We are the original story tellers of America, and we are here to reclaim our stories and join you in telling yours."

---

[7] Writers Guild of America West (WGAW) Native American and Indigenous Writers' Committee (NAIWC), "Open Letter to Hollywood," 16 October 2020, https://www.wga.org/news-events/news/connect/10-16-20/native-american-indigenous-writers-committee-releases-open-letter-to-hollywood (Accessed 28 November 2020).

Turning to the world of language-learner literature, each of the following statements represents a synthesis of many voices we have heard from a variety of people: students, parents, teachers, authors, alumni, community members in schools and in the local and global communities represented in language-learner literature.

* This book doesn't capture what life is like in [my culture]. I feel misrepresented. Is this the image that North American students are getting of my culture and my people?

* It feels weird for an outsider to be writing about us when this person has not even been to my country. Why not ask us to write our own stories?

* Why are all the stories they write about us of pain and poverty?

* Who told them they could tell that story? That story is not for them to tell.

* This story is really painful. It is not a part of my culture that we want to show off to outsiders. Did anyone ask us? Why do they keep telling the 'dirt' instead of letting us decide what stories to tell? It feels like we are being sensationalized for someone else's entertainment.

* The Spanish in this book is really awkward. The people are supposed to be from [my country], but it's not how we speak. I can barely read it and make sense of it.

* I'm not really interested in these books because they have so many White people on the covers. Where are the books about people who look like me?

* I feel disappointed because the cover of this book looked like it would be something I can relate to, but on the inside the way of seeing things doesn't seem authentic. It feels like a White person talking as if they were BIPOC.

* One more story about us told by a White person. Don't they have their own stories to tell?

* It feels as if they are shopping around for stories (from our countries) to write their books.

* First they stole our resources, now they are stealing our stories.

* Another book written with White lenses.

I really want my kid to learn about culture so they can grow up with respect for other people. That seems so important in today's political climate. Is the curriculum going to just teach language, or teach about other cultures?

You've got to be kidding. I spent money for a book that reinforces an outdated and harmful view on a country's culture? I cannot use this book with my students. How many books do I have to buy before I can get a good one that I can actually use? How am I supposed to fill up my free voluntary reading library?

How can I learn about authentic perspectives from another culture when the person writing it is from my own culture? It's like I'm reading my own culture's ways of thinking, just set in a different country.

I started this book but I don't really like it because it makes people from my country look like we're all [introduce stereotyped image].

I feel like the materials in my high school Spanish classes contributed to a problematic binary of the 'other' instead of developing an appreciation of the cultures we studied.

I urgently want to increase the amount of literature that my students can read in the target language. Their success, and my success as a teacher, depends on it.

My students seem to assume either that the whole world thinks like they do, or that other people think 'weird'. Some of these books don't help, because they have North American thinking, just using words from another language. How can I genuinely expose them to different ways of seeing the world and help them to understand other perspectives?

I want to write, and I feel called to write, but I am not sure how to do that as a White writer without stepping over boundaries somewhere. Is there a place for me to write?

PART TWO: ANALYSIS

ANALYSIS: the second stage of the observe-analyze-act cycle of social action/*praxis*.

The following is an extended critical analysis of the issues underlying the observations in Part One. It consists of an opening essay, several philosophical frameworks, and a discussion of terms and concepts.

.....

ESSAY: "Those who tell the stories rule the world."
--unknown origin[8]

Wall mural at Contently's office in New York

When we author stories, we have power. We in North America and Europe,[9] like it or not, are part of an historic imperial force that has attempted to rule the world, not only through physical and economical structures but also through structures of thought and storytelling.[10] We need to see our work as language teachers in this broader historical context of European and North American imperial exploitation and erasure of Latin American, Caribbean, African, Asian and Pacific Islands (API) and Indigenous cultures.[11] When one

---

[8] This proverb has been attributed on the internet to various Indigenous groups (Hopi, Navajo) as well as ancient Greco-Roman writers (Plato, Aristotle). Thanks to Karen Rowan in her "How to Write a CI Novel" workshop, Spring 2020, for sharing this image and quote.

[9] "Europe," here, extends to include countries formed by the British Empire or other European colonizers, such as Australia, New Zealand or South Africa, which have continued the imperial legacy. North America, in this reference, refers to the United States and Canada.

[10] French political philosopher Françoise Vergès explains about Western imperialism in *epistemology* (that is, the study of structures of thought): "Epistemic justice means that we must read, discuss, quote works from thinkers of the Global South. We must at least be aware that Western thinking is one school of thinking, that Western thought is a historical construction that has marginalized and erased not only non-European knowledge and epistemologies, but also knowledge that existed on the continent called "Europe"—women who were called "witches," nomads, the Roma people, and indigenous communities such as the Sámis. "Western" thought has been built upon erasure." Kang Kang, interview with Françoise Vergès, "To Dismantle the Master's Tools: An Interview with Françoise Vergès," *South of the South* (Issue 1), undated, https://www.timesmuseum.org/en/journal/south-of-the-south/an-interview-with-fran-oise-verg-s (accessed 7 March 2021).

[11] As Martinican scholar Aimé Césaire commented on this imperialism in the 1950s, referring to "American domination--the only domination from which one never recovers. I mean from which one never recovers unscarred." Césaire, *Discourse on Colonialism*, trans. Joan Pinkham (New York: Monthly

reads accounts of colonization, exploitation and erasure over the centuries, such as *Las venas abiertas/The Open Veins of Latin America* by Eduardo Galeano[12], it leads to a re-evaluation of how we do what we do. Are we going to folks in Latin America and the Caribbean, or Africa, or Asia and the Pacific Islands (API), or Indigenous North American communities asking for stories to serve us and our needs? That fits in with our imperial legacy of harvesting rubber, oil, bananas… and now, we extract stories and attempt to filter them through our subjective lenses when we author them in our voices.

This extraction gets even more problematic when we consider that publishing companies and authors make money off of copyrighting and selling stories from others. Have we heeded yet the words of the Puerto Rican band Calle 13 in the song that many of us teachers love: "Latinoamérica"? <<Tú no puedes comprar mi alegría, tú no puedes comprar mis dolores>>… *You can't buy my joy, you can't buy my sorrows.*[13] Unfortunately, we are doing just that when we make money off of selling stories that don't belong to us.

We also need to consider the narrative we are creating about other people. Are we making space for others to define themselves and their own story? As Gayatri Chakravorty Spivak expresses in her seminal essay, "Can the subaltern speak?"[14] When we author the stories of people from target cultures, we often reproduce historic constructs of *subalterity* in which some communities are seen as "lesser" (*sub*) and "other" (*alter*) as a result of not having adequate access to literary representation on their own terms.[15] We thus miss out on an opportunity for our students to hear the truths of others, expressed in their terms.

When we author stories of other cultures through our own North American/European, non-African, non-Indigenous, non-API and non-Latin American/Caribbean/Latinx voices, we flatten all voices to be mirrors of our own culture, reinforcing the false notion that "everyone is just like us" or "everyone should be like us." This view, however unintentional, is disrespectful and lacks humility, and mistakenly leads students to believe that Western structures of thought are universal instead of particular[16].

Review Press, 2000), 77, originally published as *Discours sur le colonialisme* (Editions Présence Africaine, 1955).

[12] Eduardo Galeano, *Open veins of Latin America: Five centuries of the pillage of a continent,* trans. by Cedric Belfrage (NYU Press, 1997), orig. pub. *Las venas abiertas de América Latina* (Madrid: Siglo Veintiuno, 1971).

[13] "Latinoamérica." Track 7 on *Entren los que quieran*. Sony Music, audio recording (4:58). Calle 13, performed with Totó la Momposina, Susana Baca, Maria Rita y Gustavo Santaolalla, 2010.

[14] Gayatri Chakravorty Spivak, "Can the Subaltern Speak?", in *Marxism and the Interpretation of Culture*, eds. Cary Nelson and Lawrence Grossberg (Urbana, IL: University of Illinois Press, 1988), 271-313.

[15] Latina / Latin American philosopher Ofelia Schutte: "The subaltern are basically those who lack access to discursive (but also political) representation on their own terms. For example, in historical narratives, accounts of indigenous uprisings are usually told on somebody else's terms." Schutte, "Philosophy, Postcoloniality, and Postmodernity," 312-326, in *A Companion to Latin American Philosophy,* eds. Susana Nuccetelli, Ofelia Schutte, and Otávio Bueno (Malden, MA: Wiley-Blackwell, 2013), 316.

[16] The harms in this centering of European and North American literary structures of thought can be illustrated by a parallel with literal architectural structures in the Caribbean, where "[i]n Guadeloupe, for

Authoring others' stories through our lenses serves to universalize our own voice[17] instead of recognizing that others have distinct ways of seeing the world--one of our instructional objectives in the Cultures strand of products, practices and perspectives in the ACTFL 5 Cs. Our students thus miss out on the deep engagement and dialogue with another cultural paradigm that might have arisen if the book were written from the voice of someone in that culture.

In this regard, I (Kristi) think of Adriana's novel, *Un nuevo amanecer* (in English, *A new dawn*).[18] Not only does her authentic Colombian voice spotlight elements of Colombian culture than a non-Colombian author might overlook--*ollas de café* (coffee pots), *el páramo* (refers to Andean mountain topography), *el frailejón* (refers to a species of Andean plant)--and incorporate phrasing not generally heard from non-native speakers--*no tiene la más mínima opción* ("does not have any option"), *una junta comunitaria* ("community board")--but the entire novel centers on a *cosmovisión andina* ("Andean cosmovision") as well as a way of storytelling that comes from one who deeply knows and *lives* that paradigm. This is a much richer intercultural experience for the reader than a book that portrays Colombia (or any other country, for that matter) from the outside.

When we write about cultures not our own, we also run the risk of deciding for them which of their stories they want to share with the outside world. Not everything is fair game for public knowledge simply because it exists. Some things are private. As Debbie Reese tells us, there is a metaphoric curtain drawn over cultures, and the right belongs to those *in* the house to decide who gets to see into the private dwelling, how, and when--if at all.

---

example, almost all of the 100 monuments classified to date – military buildings, churches and cathedrals, homes and estates, sugar and coffee mills and factories, all striking symbols of colonial power – feature European architecture. The same can be said for UNESCO World Heritage sites. The 12 listed cultural sites in the Caribbean, for example, are all examples of colonial architecture. Local people often have a hard time identifying with such places, which remind them less of the lives of their ancestors than of the power of their masters." Whether concrete building structures or abstract structures of thought, a similar erasure and harm occurs with centering European and North American constructions. Local Caribbean groups have been decentering the European historical sites by "creat[ing] places of memory and reveal[ing] remnants of the past that hold identity and even emotion," a development which "has allowed African Americans to unearth the legacy of their ancestors, filled with memory and connection." This runs parallel with the power of #OwnVoices to create literature that holds authentic identity, memory and connection. See André Delpuech, "Colonisation and Slavery: For a Necessary and Rightful Place in Heritage and Museums," International Council of Museums, 19 January 2021, https://icom.museum/en/news/colonisation-and-slavery-archaeology/ (accessed 7 March 2021).

[17] "Presenting as 'multicultural' material that was actually generated by and is representative of White, NES [native English-speaking] Americans has the effect of reinforcing normative constructs of all cultures as White." Suhanthie Motha, *Race, empire, and English language teaching: Creating responsible and ethical anti-racist practice* (New York: Teachers College Press, 2014), 105. For the purposes of this book, as discussed in the "Terms" section, we expand "White" to the terms "nmTC" and/or "Imperial." Motha's point resounds about the universalization of our own voices when we author others' stories.

[18] Adriana is a co-author of this book, but she did not suggest this part! This was authored apart from her prior knowledge.

We also run the risk of telling a single story. As Chimamanda Ngozi Adichie powerfully expressed in her 2009 TEDTalk, "The Danger of a Single Story,"[19] the "single story" happens when storytellers generalize about a culture such that *all* people in that culture are portrayed as sharing a single experience, instead of recognizing the diversity of experiences within a culture.

In addition, the "single story" that we tell is often, albeit unintentionally, skewed to benefit those systems that have perpetuated oppression. As a classic African proverb says, "Until the lion tells his side of the story, the tale of the hunt will always glorify the hunter."[20]

Many of us are on board with these reflections, especially in light of the #OwnVoices[21] and #DignidadLiteraria[22] movements which have gained prominence in the wake of the January 2020 publication of *American Dirt*--an Oprah's Book Club novel in which a White U.S. author Jeanine Cummins attempted to represent the voice of a Mexican character migrating to the United States. These hashtag movements, situated in widespread cultural reckonings around racism and the increasing emergence of the "decolonial turn,"[23] have led to a powerful collective reflection in many loci of global power. The world language teaching community wrestles with how to apply these reflections to our own contexts, and we grapple with ongoing internal critical self-questioning of our practices regarding cultural appropriation and the extent to which we respect and honor cultures and the voices of communities from target cultures. As we engage in this self-questioning, we feel acutely the profound need for a wide range of comprehensible stories, particularly for our novice-level students; we don't want to sacrifice our emerging ideals, yet we also urgently need comprehensible stories.

---

[19] Chimamanda Ngozi Adichie, "The Danger of a Single Story" (2009), TEDGlobal 2009, https://www.ted.com/talks/chimamanda_ngozi_adichie_the_danger_of_a_single_story/transcript (accessed 15 June 2020).

[20] Thank you to Dr. Cécile Acclien for suggesting the inclusion of this proverb and sharing with us that it has been attributed to many different African cultures.

[21] See further discussion of #OwnVoices in Framework 7 ("#OwnVoices") of this book.

[22] #DignidadLiteraria / #LiteraryDignity was founded in January 2020 by Myriam Gurba, David Bowles and Roberto Lovato as "a network of committed Latinx authors formed to combat the invisibility of Latinx authors, editors and executives in the U.S. publishing industry and the dearth of Latinx literature on the shelves of America's bookstores and libraries. #DignidadLiteraria believes in the social and political power of wholly authentic Latinx voices and that it is the duty of the publishing industry and literati to use their full power and privilege to elevate these voices." See further discussion in Framework 7 ("#OwnVoices) of this book. Source: DignidadLiteraria, "*#DignidadLiteraria press conference*," 2020, https://dignidadliteraria.com (accessed 27 November 2020).

[23] The phrase "decolonial turn," or *el giro descolonial,* was coined in 2005 by Puerto Rican philosopher Nelson Maldonado-Torres: "The decolonial turn does not refer to a single theoretical school, but rather points to a family of diverse positions that share a view of coloniality as a fundamental problem in the modern (as well as postmodern and information) age, and of decolonization or decoloniality as a necessary task that remains unfinished." In Maldonado-Torres, "Thinking through the decolonial turn: Post-continental interventions in theory, philosophy, and critique—An introduction," *Transmodernity: Journal of Peripheral Cultural Production of the Luso-Hispanic World* 1.2 (2011), 2, https://dialnet.unirioja.es/descarga/articulo/3979025.pdf, accessed 27 November 2020.

How might we have gotten into this pattern of authoring other people's stories?

Filtering the experiences of members of target cultures through the lenses of an oppressor culture has long existed as part of the dynamic of colonization, which has profoundly shaped each of us who has benefitted from the privileges it has afforded us, whether in terms of language, customs, religion, economics, health and safety, access to opportunities and resources, and more.

However, within the world language teaching community, many of us explicitly desire to disrupt the patterns that tend to subjugate people from the cultures that speak the languages that we teach. It's often a reason why we got into this profession in the first place. We want to create a world of more mutual respect, peace and justice through languages. However, we are still influenced by the mindset of the oppressor culture in which we live and were raised, and also by an outdated model of technology and communication.

We who belong to the demographic that is the principal audience for this book—language teachers who are not members of the cultures whose languages we teach—have, for much of the history of our profession, regarded *ourselves* as the "cultural bridges." Many of us have followed a common trajectory: we traveled abroad, immersed ourselves in a language, heard many stories that shaped our worldview, then returned to our home communities as ambassadors, eager to share another language and other perspectives. It's logical, then, in that context, that we would find ourselves believing that it fell on us to author the stories of people from other countries. If we had stopped to question this celebrated role as ambassador--something many of us probably only rarely did, if ever--we probably would have expressed that we did not have the practical means to do otherwise, short of lengthy pen pal processes, painstaking and expensive cross-continental collaborations, or bringing in visitors from another culture. This, of course, is not the experience of all language educators of this demographic, but it is a common trajectory and experience.

With the advent of the internet, however, we who are not members of the cultures whose languages we teach need to rethink our paradigm and role. We must acknowledge that in trying to be a *bridge,* we have been a cultural *filter,* inevitably projecting our cultural lenses on the stories we are trying to "authentically" communicate.[24] In an earlier era, we may have felt we had few other options. However, this model is no longer our best practice; it is largely obsolete now that many people from all over the planet have the technological means to communicate their stories directly.[25]

---

[24] "We make sense of perceptions and experiences through our particular cultural lens. This lens is neither universal nor objective…" Robin diAngelo, *White Fragility: Why it's so hard for White people to talk about racism* (Boston: Beacon, 2018), 9.

[25] See, for example, Doña Angela's "De Mi Rancho a Tu Cocina," a cooking show she broadcasts directly from her ranch in Michoacán, México. Since its debut in September 2019, her show has amassed over 2.87 million followers on YouTube (as of 26 June 2020). https://www.youtube.com/channel/UCJjyyWFwUIOfKhb35WgCqVg/videos (accessed 26 June 2020).

Furthermore, we must shift our paradigm from one that regards **target cultures (TCs) that speak the target language (TL)** as *international* to one that sees that TCs as *national, regional and local,* since communities of **members of target cultures (mTCs)** are often present in our own neighborhoods and families. We live in multilingual and multicultural nations. This shift is especially salient for educators who are White or otherwise associated with dominant privilege, who were often conditioned socially to either overlook the presence of mTCs in their own hometowns, or to instinctively regard them as subaltern and somehow deficient, as if they did not possess the necessary skills to bring stories and content to students. That era of overt and covert White supremacy must be dismantled[26] and we must play a conscious role in the struggle, actively constructing classrooms of equity in which we invite and center voices of mTCs, whether from local, regional, national or international contexts. The second half of this work will provide concrete examples of how such collaboration can occur in the creation of language-learner literature.

Why might so many in our profession persist in the problematic practice of authoring other people's stories?

While perhaps some teachers have not begun the critical questioning described above, many of us have. Yet many in our profession persist in authoring other people's stories for several possible reasons, including: 1) We are still shifting into the above-described new paradigm about possibilities for communication afforded to us by technological advances. 2) We are profoundly affected by dynamics of colonization, privilege and oppression on an international and local level, including in our own classrooms--dynamics in which most of us are complicit. This includes existing structures of segregation that have prevented many people from forming the egalitarian cross-cultural relationships that they might wish to form. 3) We need resources that are authentically #OwnVoices from mTCs *and* provide the repetitive, comprehensible input that learners need. There is a dearth of #OwnVoices stories from mTCs at a novice and intermediate-low level. 4) Furthermore, while experiencing this lack of material, we feel the push to meet the ACTFL World-Readiness Standards, also known as "The 5Cs": we need to fulfill not just the standards for language/**C**ommunication, but also for **C**ultures, **C**omparisons, **C**onnections, **C**ommunities[27]. We feel a profound responsibility to our stakeholders to fulfill these standards. If we were to generate authentic material from our own context--for example, a book written in the TL about one of the many ubiquitous drive-through coffee kiosks in Western Washington State--we might face criticism from colleagues, students/parents, administrators for not "teaching culture." So, we persist in

---

[26] This book was initially drafted before the world-shaking events surrounding the death of George Floyd from police brutality. Massive changes with regard to conscientization about racial injustice are unfolding, and this book seeks to contribute a "grano de arena" (grain of sand) to this great groundswell of mobilization through our particular context of world language education.

[27] American Council on the Teaching of Foreign Languages, "World-Readiness Standards for Learning Languages" (2015), https://www.actfl.org/sites/default/files/publications/standards/World-ReadinessStandardsforLearningLanguages.pdf (accessed 26 June 2020).

authoring other people's stories because we don't have enough #OwnVoices language-learner literature from mTCs to meet our professional obligations. 5) We also persist because many of us feel a strong desire to exercise our gifts as writers. There are likely many other additional reasons that could be explored.

A natural solution to the problem of telling other peoples' stories is to increase the amount of #OwnVoices literature produced by members of target cultures (mTCs). Yet, as mentioned, this often leaves the teacher who is a **non-member of a target culture (nmTC)** wondering: "Is there a place for me to use my storytelling gifts? How do I create a Free Voluntary Reading library in the meantime while waiting for more #OwnVoices language-learner stories from mTCs?"

In response to these questions above, this book proposes the following paths for writers from North America and Europe and other loci of global imperial power who are not members of cultures that speak the languages they teach, who want to be involved in the creation of language-learner literature, and seek to honor and respect #OwnVoices storytelling from members of target cultures for the development of interculturality in students.

Before we describe the paths, let's continue with the analysis by taking a look at the underlying philosophical frameworks of the paths and this work, and some definitions of terms and concepts.

Identifying Philosophical Frameworks

Framework 1: Navigating social classification structures of racialization, coloniality, and linguistic-target-culture

In contemplating the issues surrounding literary (mis)representation in language-learner literature, we have conceived and reconceived this project through the lenses of various social classification structures, charted below. Each structure encompasses a spectrum represented with conceptual poles and intermediary hybrid space (indicated by the symbol ← →).

	Pole A		Pole B
Structure: Racialization	people of color (Black, Indigenous, People of Color)	← →	people of whiteness
Structure: (De)coloniality	members of historically and currently colonized nations and communities	← →	members of historically and currently colonizing nations of global power (i.e. empires)
Structure: Linguistic-Target-Culture	members of a particular target culture* that speaks the target language being taught *Cultural membership includes those who belong to a culture and do not speak the target language of that culture, such as English-only Latinxs.	← →	non-members of a particular target culture that speaks the target language being taught

Upon continued reflection, we have identified our principal structure for analyzing literary (mis)representation as that of colonial imperialism, a dynamic which can be perpetuated by people regardless of racialized identity (although imperialism is deeply entwined with whiteness) and can be perpetuated by people regardless of linguistic-target-culture identity.

Notwithstanding this principal structure, our main intended audience is comprised of people who will self-identify as residing on Pole B on this chart in all three structures: racialized, (de)colonial, and linguistic-target-culture. For example, a White person from the U.S. whose first language is English and who is not Latinx would likely overlap with all three Pole B structures in the diagram above. The main reason for this choice of main intended audience is that this is currently the principal demographic of the world language teachers and authors in North America.

Our secondary audience includes people who may identify as Pole A on all three structures, or a mix of Poles A and B, and find themselves at risk of misrepresenting another group of people in literature.

These structures above are not tidy. They are complicated even further by the fact that many identities reside as a hybrid between two (or possibly more) poles in any one of these structures. (For instance, one can identify as both a member and a non-member of a culture, or identify as both a BIPOC and White, or be simultaneously colonized and colonizer.)

To untangle these complexities would require a work with a much larger scope than this one. We are sitting with the complexity. As mentioned above, we are centering one structure as our primary lens for analysis--the (de)colonial structure--while variably utilizing terminology from all three constructs, depending on the nature of the specific points we are making.

For further discussion on the terminology, please visit the section "Defining Terms and Concepts."

Framework 2: The acquisition of respectful interculturality as an end goal

The title of this book refers to "the acquisition of respectful interculturality." But what does that mean? As mentioned earlier in this book, the United Nations Educational, Scientific and Cultural Organization (UNESCO) describes *interculturality* as "the existence and equitable interaction of diverse cultures and the possibility of generating shared cultural expressions through dialogue and mutual respect."[28] *Respectful interculturality* captures the heart of this definition with a special highlight on the aspect of mutual respect.

Interculturality has emerged in the last few decades as an area for renewed focus within the world language profession, as evidenced by the NCSSFL-ACTFL Can-Do Statements for Intercultural Communication (2017)[29] [30] and the NCSSFL-ACTFL

---

[28] United Nations Educational, Scientific and Cultural Organization (UNESCO), "Interculturality," https://en.unesco.org/creativity/interculturality (accessed September 15, 2020).

[29] It is interesting to note that various documents surrounding the NCSSFL-ACTFL Can-Do Statements for Intercultural Communication, such as publications at various state levels, refer to "[inter]cultural competence." Debate about this term has been reviewed by public health educators Ella Greene-Moton and Meredith Minkler in "Cultural Competence or Cultural Humility? Moving Beyond the Debate," *SAGE Pub*, 12 November 2019, https://doi.org/10.1177/1524839919884912 [Accessed 28 November 2020]). Readers may be interested to review the reflections from various voices around the terms *[inter]cultural competence* and *[inter]cultural humility*, especially as these perspectives may affect the way we articulate our goals for students and collectively envision the concept of respectful interculturality.

[30] NCSSFL-ACTFL Can-Do Statements: Proficiency Benchmarks (2017), https://www.actfl.org/sites/default/files/can-dos/Intercultural%20Can-Do_Statements.pdf (Accessed 28 November 2020).

Intercultural Communication Reflection Tool.[31] World language educators who teach by means of stories have sought to teach interculturality through stories set in the contexts of target cultures in which the target language is predominantly spoken.

In this endeavor to teach interculturality through stories, however, our materials have sometimes centered more on the comprehensibility of the language--via cognates and repetitions of high-frequency words--than on the genuinely *respectful* interculturality[32] that we seek to foster. We have a responsibility to foster both language acquisition AND the acquisition of genuine, respectful interculturality. This book seeks to empower our world language profession toward a greater realization of these tandem goals through participation in the production of new language-learner literature to help students to know themselves[33] and others more authentically--the basis of this respectful interculturality.

With regard to the term "respectful," it is important to note that what a person from one culture may feel is "respectful" may not be felt as respectful by someone from another culture. The subjective perception of "respectful" underscores the need for ongoing open dialogue across all groups involved in a particular interaction or project, with particular preference given to the subjective perceptions of those groups who have historically held less power in colonial social structures.

Framework 3: "Staying in Our Lanes": A Metaphor

The notion of "staying in our lanes," which we use in the Staying in Our Lanes Project and which applies to this book, functions as a response to the pop culture phrase "stay in your lane," which usually connotes "mind your own business." While this pop phrase may sound harsh to some listeners, it aligns with the message from communities who are asking outsiders to respect their autonomy about how/when/whether to tell their own stories.[34] The phrase "staying in our lanes" thus signifies that we who are White and/or Empire-identified *are listening* to voices from marginalized communities who are asking us to "stay in our lanes" as part of our commitment to racial and social justice,[35]

---

[31] NCSSFL-ACTFL Intercultural Communication Reflection Tool, https://www.actfl.org/sites/default/files/can-dos/Intercultural%20Can-Dos_Reflections%20Scenarios.pdf (Accessed 28 November 2020).

[32] By *interculturality*, we mean something broader than *internationality*. Interculturality also happens between people of different subcultural identities, such as different cliques in schools that come to understand each other.

[33] The novice-level book *Brandon Brown Quiere un Perro* [*Brandon Brown Wants a Dog*] by Carol Gaab (Denver, CO: Fluency Matters, 2013) is a classic example of a book that helps readers to know themselves. It holds a mirror to students' own love for animals and their ethical reasoning about truth-telling and keeping secrets. First knowing oneself is essential for later revealing oneself to others across (sub)cultures.

[34] See, for example, the hashtags #DiversityJedi, #WeNeedDiverseBooks, #DignidadLiteraria, #OwnVoices; see also the Open Letters from Latinx, Black and Native/Indigenous screenwriters in Part I.

[35] See, for example, racial educator Catrice M. Jackson, "'Get In Your Lane Anti-Racism Workshop," *Catriceology,* undated (copyright 2015-2020), Accessed 13 July 2020, http://www.catriceology.com/get-in-your-lane-workshop; Ashton P. Woods, "Hey White People, Stay in Your Lane!", *#TheBlog,* 23 April 2017, Accessed 13 July 2020, https://www.ashtonpwoods.com/theblog/hey-white-

and *responding* by calling in our own social groups to a conversation about how we can do better with how we use, share and yield power within our context of storytelling for language learners. This benefits everyone involved, as it leads us all more strongly into intercultural relationships of mutual sharing and respect--a primary goal of world language education.

The phrase "staying in our lanes" may provoke discomfort for some readers. We encourage readers to sit with any discomfort and approach the emotion with curiosity. In the words of White novelist Katie Robison,

> "I've learned a lot about how to be a better writer and ally, and I've thought a great deal about the position (and privilege) I occupy in society and how that's reflected in my work. If I had to summarize what I've learned into a single sentence, it would probably be: Stay in your lane. I resisted that idea a lot at the beginning of the year, but I've come to understand why it's so important."[36]

We intend, through this book, to shed a light on why "staying in our lanes" is so important for guiding us and our students into more mutually nourishing, collaborative, and empathetic relationships across and within cultures, through new paths for creative flourishing as we pursue writing toward the acquisition of respectful interculturality.

Some may fear that the concept of "staying in our lanes" promotes division and segregation. On the contrary, we envision a shared space in which everyone *makes space* and *takes space*, creating an opportunity for *all* to be seen and heard, fostering greater unity and deepened communal relationships. In that vein, "Staying in Our Lanes" invokes images of highway travel to envision a shared space in which multiple people travel toward their goals, in harmony. This shared space functions by each "driver" respecting the boundaries of what actions and leadership lie within their domain by virtue of their identities, and which are best conceded to the agency and leadership of others.

"Staying in our lanes" thus means "making space" and "taking space," knowing when to speak and when to stay silent. In the context of world language teaching, it fosters trust and collaboration among people of different identities toward our shared goals of peace, justice, and friendship--respectful interculturality--through language and literacy education. It connotes positive, hopeful images of avenues forward and paths to follow.

"Staying in our lanes," as used in this book, is directed toward people in loci of imperial power. It amplifies the voices of those calling for global decolonization as it calls for recognition of respectful boundaries, in contrast with the invasive spirit of colonization.

For more reflection, see "FAQ: Why do we stress 'staying in our lanes' so fervently?" in the Q&A section toward the end of this book.

---

people-stay-in-your-lane; Olúfẹ́mi Táíwò, "Don't Stand With Me," *Blog of the APA [American Psychological Association]*, 30 June 2020, Accessed 13 July 2020, https://blog.apaonline.org/2020/06/30dont-stand-with-me/.

[36] Katie Robison, "Final Thoughts: Stay in Your Lane," *Katie Robison,* 8 October 2017, Accessed 13 July 2020, https://katierobison.com/improving-representation-final-thoughts/

Framework 4: Stories that "belong" to others / Deep culture

What does it mean for a story to "belong" to someone? Clearly, one's own life story belongs to that person. But in what sense does a story belong to a whole community or a culture? The chart below illustrates the fruits of the authors' conversations about this.

Story doesn't necessarily "belong" to a culture Story has a lower level of embeddedness in the culture.	Story "belongs" to a culture Story has a higher level of embeddedness in the culture.
- minimal cultural references - easily transferable to a different place because the setting and props are peripheral to the themes and plot of the story	- setting is in the foreground - cultural practices - perspectives behind practices and products - sacred and religious and ritual themes - symbols - histories - ancestors and heroes - folktales & legends* - folk songs* - anything connected to pain - "behind the curtain" (see Framework 6) - deep culture: "tacit knowledge and unconscious assumptions that govern our worldview…." (Hammond, *Culturally-Responsive Teaching*, 23) - folk culture *It should be noted, in particular, that many folk songs, folktales and legends, as well as other genres, are intended by a culture to be orally transmitted, and outsiders can do great harm when attempting to put them into print. The oral tradition has great intergenerational power for a community, and only the community itself can authorize a transition from orality to textuality with regard to a particular story or song.*

In discussing the extensive nature of what "belongs" to a culture, it helps to consider the "iceberg" model of culture[37], a model which is likely familiar to many readers.

---

[37] The iceberg model comes from many sources. This particular image is available at http://opengecko.com/interculturalism/visualising-the-iceberg-model-of-culture/ (Accessed 18 July 2020).

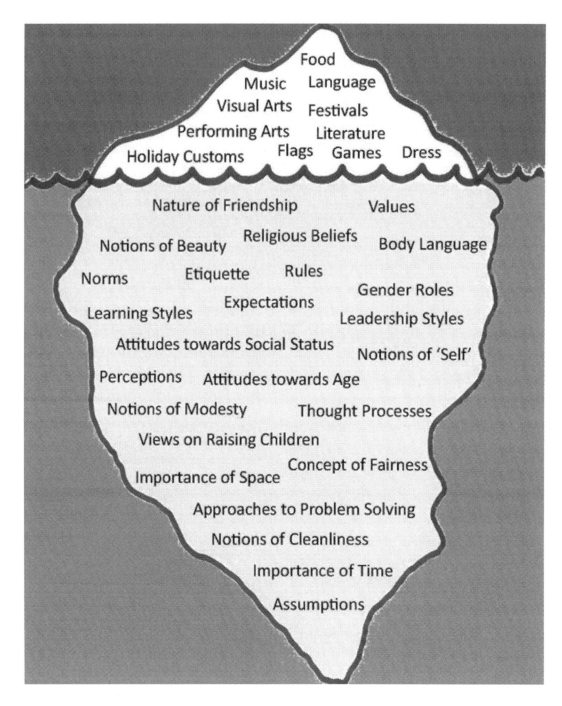

We authors all agree that the "deep" aspects of culture under the waterline, as *perspectives*, belong to that culture and need to be represented in literature by members of that culture, not non-members. We also believe that the majority of so-called "surface" (externally visible) aspects of culture would also be up to members of that culture to choose to represent, as they involve cultural *practices* that belong to them. It is theoretically possible that some of the *products* (e.g. food, flags, pop music) could appear as props in literature written by an external observer, to the extent that the products are made to be shared with or seen by outsiders, but choice to portray the *perspectives* behind those products would belong to members of the target culture.

This iceberg model points out the vast amount of themes that are involved in a discussion of culture and which go deep into the human psyche, forming "deep culture." Intercultural educator Zaretta Hammond explains,

> "[Deep culture] is made up of tacit knowledge and unconscious assumptions that govern our worldview. It also contains the cosmology (view of good or bad) that guides ethics, spirituality, health, and theories of group harmony (i.e., competition or cooperation). Deep culture also governs how we learn new information. Elements at this level have an intense emotional charge. Mental models at this level help the brain interpret threats or rewards in the environment. Challenges to cultural values at this level produce culture shock or trigger the brain's fight or flight response.
>
> "At the deep cultural level, our brain is encoding itself with the particular worldview we will carry into our formative years. Two people from different cultures can look at the same event and have very different reactions to it because of the meaning they attach to the event based on their deep culture."[38]

As Hammond explains, deep culture exists deep within the psyche as the worldview that each person forms during their early years of life. If you're not a member of the culture, it's not possible for you to represent deep culture. As such, a non-member of a particular target culture needs to respect the limitations of their own cognitive constructs and let members of that target culture represent their deep culture, including their practices and perspectives which may differ from others who share the same culture.

Why we should NOT author stories that belong to others:

In short, there are two broad reasons.
1. <u>Different subjectivities</u>: As Hammond explains above, by virtue of our language and culture, we have different subjective cognitive categories than people of another language and culture. We will therefore inevitably project our subjective worldviews onto a protagonist of another culture.
2. <u>Dismantling colonialism</u>: As we discuss in the next section, those of us who represent historic and current colonizer countries owe justice to colonized communities by not appropriating their stories, as this perpetuates oppression.

In summary, sometimes we need to not author someone else's story for reasons of differing cultural subjectivities (non-member of a particular target culture vs. member of a

---

[38] Zaretta Hammond, *Culturally Responsive Teaching and The Brain: Promoting Authentic Engagement and Rigor Among Culturally and Linguistically Diverse Students* (Thousand Oaks, CA: Corwin, 2014), 23.

particular target culture), sometimes for reasons of dismantling colonialism (colonizer vs. colonized), and sometimes for both reasons.

What are the risks when we do attempt to author the stories of others?

The following is a non-exhaustive sampling of some of the harms that can inadvertently result when authors write stories that do not belong to them:

- **perpetuation of stereotypes and racist tropes**

- **telling a "single story"**[39]

- **missionary / White savior mentality:** as if members of target cultures (mTCs) that speak the target language needed "saving" or rescuing by non-members of the target culture (nmTC) instead of having the agency and capacity to address their own needs[40]

- **reification of a Western worldview:** as if a Western worldview were universal and culture-transcendent, applicable throughout time and space, instead of particular and contextual[41]

- **paternalism:** as if mTC from colonized communities were lesser and childlike, with flattened character development and simplistic attributes, and in need of enlightenment by Empire-identified characters

---

[39] See Chimimanda Ngozi Adichie's seminal TED Talk (2009), "The Danger of a Single Story," [video, 18:34] https://www.ted.com/talks/chimamanda_ngozi_adichie_the_danger_of_a_single_story?language=en. Adichie on the single story: "So that is how to create a single story, show a people as one thing, as only one thing, over and over again, and that is what they become. It is impossible to talk about the single story without talking about power. There is a word, an Igbo word, that I think about whenever I think about the power structures of the world, and it is "nkali." It's a noun that loosely translates to "to be greater than another." Like our economic and political worlds, stories too are defined by the principle of *nkali*: How they are told, who tells them, when they're told, how many stories are told, are really dependent on power. Power is the ability not just to tell the story of another person, but to make it the definitive story of that person" (9:18-10:07).

[40] Note that, historically, colonization by violent force has typically been followed by colonization of the interior life through the imposition of the colonizers' religion through missionary activity. This commentary is not intended to be hostile to religion per se, but to stimulate reflection about its collusion with oppression. The emerging field of postcolonial religious studies may interest some readers.

The much-criticized field of voluntourism also perpetuates this "savior" mentality while doing harm to communities. See, for example, the discussion around "Savior Barbie": Lily Kuo, "Instagram's White Savior Barbie neatly captures what's wrong with 'voluntourism' in Africa," Quartz Africa, 20 April 2016, https://qz.com/africa/665764/instagrams-white-savior-barbie-neatly-captures-whats-wrong-with-voluntourism-in-africa/ (accessed 7 March 2021).

[41] For a discussion of the historic development of the notion of universal knowledge produced by men from a handful of European nations, see Ramón Grosfoguel, "The structure of knowledge in westernized universities: Epistemic racism/sexism and the four genocides/epistemicides," *Human Architecture: Journal of the sociology of self-knowledge* 1 (2013), 73-90, https://scholarworks.umb.edu/cgi/viewcontent.cgi?article=1445&context=humanarchitecture (accessed 17 July 2020).

- **absolutism:** as if it were possible to describe mTC with "always"/"never" binaries and other absolutes, instead of with nuanced and varied descriptors

- **objectification:** as if mTCs from colonized cultures were objects to be treated according to the whims of Empire-identified members, instead of possessing their own subjective interests

- **fetishization and exotification:** as if mTCs were "so cool" and "so interesting" instead of ordinary people living human journeys to the best of their ability; a mentality as if a connection to an mTC raised the "cool" status of the nmTC.

- **White hero / victim paradigm:** as if White people were always the hero or the victim, and never the villain, in a narrative[42]

- **instrumentalism:** as if other people and cultures served to fulfill the self-actualization needs of the nmTC protagonist

- **sensationalism:** writing provocative and/or negative stories about mTCs in order to arouse a desired reader reaction, at the cost of flattening the full humanity--with joys and sorrows mixed together--of the subject[43]

- **erasure of non-dominant perspectives:** When a nmTC author writes from the perspective of a mTC character, the voice and perspective of the particular nmTC writer are usually inadvertently projected onto the mTC character, thus "erasing" particular mTC paradigms.[44]

---

[42] Kim Crayton, "Stop Recommending #WhiteFragility as a #AntiRacist Resource" (video), 2:00-2:08, https://www.pscp.tv/w/1BdxYnjQklMKX.

[43] "All of these stories [joyful and sorrowful] make me who I am. But to insist on only these negative stories is to flatten my experience and to overlook the many other stories that formed me." - Chimamanda Ngozi Adichie, "The Danger of a Single Story," TEDTalk (2009), Video [18:34], https://www.ted.com/talks/chimamandangozi_adichie_the_danger_of_a_single_story?language=en,12:49-13:02.

[44] Thanks to world language colleague Tashia Buccioni for describing this point, as well as sharing excerpts from linguist and language colleague Suhanthie Motha, who asserts that books that are ostensibly "multicultural" but are written by non-members of target cultures "operate as an assimilationist mechanism. Students pick up a book with the expectation of encountering a racial [or cultural] minority character, but instead they learn how dark-skinned faces should fit into a White world" (86) --or in our case, how members of a specific target culture are imagined by an authors who are outsiders to that culture. This assimilation is like coloring in the face of a White character to make them a Black or Brown character, as if cultures went no deeper than a skin tone (104). See Suhanthie Motha, *Race, empire, and English language teaching: Creating responsible and ethical anti-racist practice* (New York: Teachers College Press, 2014).

Unfortunately, when we who are non-members of a specific target culture attempt to write perspectives of members of that target culture, we operate in the ways Motha describes: because the categories of our thinking are deeply shaped by our culture, even subconsciously, we inadvertently take our own paradigms and situate them in the mind of a character in the target culture, due to the complex

When we do an audit of the material in our libraries of literature that has been written for language learners over the past several decades, we find many examples of the negative processes described above, regardless of the authors' best intentions. Here, as in so many arenas, what matters is addressing the harmful impacts, not focusing on the extent to which the author had good intentions.

Despite our good intentions, almost all of us have made mistakes as we author or promote material with some of the problems identified in this section. Yet, as in the famous quote attributed to Maya Angelou: "Do the best you can until you know better. Then when you know better, do better."[45] We as a community are on this continual path of reflection and changing our practices to "do better."

Although writing literature from our own (sub)cultures, as proposed by Path A later in this book, may not entirely eliminate the harmful processes described above, we are much less likely to engage in those practices when dealing with characters whose worldviews we know intimately (as they are our own).

Framework 5: Studies in Global Colonialism and Critical Theory

The concepts in this book reflect global decolonial thought and critical theories[46], movements in academia and in broader society which have emerged strongly in the last fifty years. These movements have arisen from grassroots community organizing, as greater avenues for self-expression have opened up to members of groups historically marginalized by reigning structures. They may feel new and potentially threatening to some readers who may not have been exposed to them; however, these concepts serve the purpose of liberation of communities that have historically experienced oppression. They shape contemporary discourse and will continue to shape our work as K-12 educators. These concepts also are standards by which many of our students will judge the education they've received from us as they go forth into university and look back upon what we gave them in their K-12 language instruction. We have a social responsibility to our students to do the best we can with what we know, and to push ourselves to stay current with these movements in intercultural studies.

Moreover, we owe it to the communities whose languages we teach, and--if those communities are not our home communities--to our home communities, to align ourselves with movements of liberation. Liberation for some leads to the liberation of all.

What we are proposing is *not a subtraction but an addition*: Something to increase bonds of trust and mutuality, and interconnected relationships in the world language classroom and beyond. Something that leads to greater justice and liberation that serves

---

and inescapable ways in which our cognition is shaped by culture. This contributes to the erasure of the paradigms of others.

[45] There are many movements suggesting ways to "do better," such as those recommended in the Recommended Resources section of this book.

[46] Some recommended authors: Please see the "Recommended Resources" section of this book.

all communities. Something that fills our deepest aspirations and values as teachers of language and interculturality, far beyond the oppressive structures and practices of the status quo.

Dismantling colonialism and colonization is a central theme woven throughout this book. For related definitions, see the section "Defining Terms and Concepts." For recommended reading, see Appendix III.

As pointed out in Framework 4 ("Stories that Belong to Others + The Problems We Perpetuate"), when we author stories that are not our own, we are bound to misrepresent others; when this occurs in the context of historic power dynamics of colonization, we also unwittingly reinforce structures of oppression. Chilean cultural critic Nelly Richard asserts that "given the asymmetrical power relations between North and South, the former enjoys a privileged position in its capacity to define the latter and thereby to misrepresent the other according to its own interests…".[47] For language teachers to work toward dismantling these power inequalities, we need to step out of our privilege to make space for others to define and represent themselves or "pull back the curtain" on their cultures.

Framework 6: Mirrors, Windows, Sliding Glass Doors, and Curtains in Multicultural Literature

Dr. Rudine Sims Bishop, African American professor emeritus described as the "mother of multicultural children's literature,"[48] has described literature as offering the reader a **window**, a **sliding-glass door**, and/or a **mirror**.

> *"Books are sometimes **windows**, offering views of worlds that may be real or imagined, familiar, or strange. These windows are also **sliding glass doors**, and readers have only to walk through in imagination to become part of whatever world has been created and recreated by the author. When lighting conditions are just right, however, a window can also be a **mirror**. Literature transforms the human experience and reflects it back to us in that reflection we can see our own lives and experiences as part of the larger human experience. Reading, then, becomes a means of self-affirmation, and readers often seek their mirrors in books."*[49] (bold print added)

Bishop's colleague in the field of children's literature, Dr. Debbie Reese (Nambé Pueblo tribal enrollment), has expanded on the concepts of windows, mirrors and sliding-

---

[47] Nelly Richard, summarized in Ofelia Schutte, "Philosophy, Postcoloniality, and Postmodernity," 312-326, in *A Companion to Latin American Philosophy,* eds. Susana Nuccetelli, Ofelia Schutte, and Otávio Bueno (Malden, MA: Wiley-Blackwell, 2013), 324.

[48] Robin Chenoweth, "Rudine Sims Bishop: 'Mother of Multicultural Children's Literature'," Ohio State University, 5 September 2019, https://ehe.osu.edu/news/listing/rudine-sims-bishop-diverse-childrens-books/ (accessed 10 June 2020).

[49] Rudine Sims Bishop, "Mirrors, Windows, and Sliding Glass Doors," *Perspectives: Choosing and Using Books for the Classroom* 6.3 (Summer 1990).

glass doors, suggesting the notion of **curtains**: protective coverings that a culture may pull shut or open to decide whether or not others may look in.

> "As a child, I was taught what can—and cannot—be shared with outsiders. A history of exploitation has made Native writers mindful of what they disclose.
>
> "To capture this concept, I have been adding a 'curtain' to Bishop's (1990) 'mirrors, windows, and sliding glass doors' metaphor when I talk or write about Native stories. This is a way to acknowledge and honor the stories behind the **curtain**—those that are purposefully kept within Native communities. Native communities resisted historical oppression and continue to preserve our culture by cultivating our ways in private spaces—behind the curtain. While Native people share some of our ways publicly in the present day, there is a great deal that we continue to protect from outsiders. Furthermore, it conveys the importance of how #OwnVoices knows what belongs within the community and what knowledge can be shared outside of our communities." [50]

Throughout this book, we utilize the models of windows, mirrors[51] and curtains in discussing the creation of language-learner literature for acquisition of both language and respectful interculturality.

Framework 7: #OwnVoices

> "Historically speaking, it's extremely common for marginalized characters to be written by authors who aren't part of that marginalized group and who are clueless despite having good intentions. As a result, many portrayals are lacking at best and damaging at worst. Society tends to favor privileged voices even regarding a situation they have zero experience with, and thus those are the authors that get published...
>
> "I talk about #ownvoices novels and avoid using the term #ownvoices authors. Some authors identify as such because they choose to only write about characters from their own marginalized group; that's great. Many

---

[50] Debbie Reese, "Critical Indigenous Literacies: Selecting and Using Children's Books about Indigenous Peoples," *Language Arts* 95.6 (2018), 390-391.

[51] As an example of the power of mirrors in literature for language learners, language educator Dr. Krishauna Hines-Gaither writes, "As an African American language learner, I consistently sought connections to my lived experiences. Never seeing myself represented in the course content made it challenging to find these points of convergence. Of the dozens of language classes that I took, I only recall two instances when an instructor incorporated a lesson on Black experiences...it is telling that I still recall the titles, readings, authors, and the way that they made me feel; finally, there was content that spoke to my soul." Hines-Gaither, "Anti-Racism in the World Language Classroom," *WorldView: A Language Blog*, Concordia Language Villages, 14 July 2020, http://www.concordialanguagevillages.org/blog/villages/anti-racism-in-the-world-language-classroom#.Xw8PmC3Mw6V (Accessed 15 July 2020).

authors, however, may write some books that fall into #ownvoices, and some that don't."

--Corinne Duyvis, author of young adult literature and original creator of the #OwnVoices hashtag[52]

"#OwnVoices stories [is] a hashtag created by Corinne Duyvis to describe a book that is written by someone who is of the particular culture being depicted. The idea is that the quality of a story is improved when the person creating that story is an insider who knows what to share and how to share it with outsiders. As a child, I was taught what can—and cannot—be shared with outsiders. A history of exploitation has made Native writers mindful of what they disclose."

--Dr. Debbie Reese[53]

A work is #OwnVoices when the author and protagonist share a marginalized identity. They might not share all aspects of identity.[54] #OwnVoices does not mean that supporting characters cannot have an identity different from the author. In fact, supporting characters likely *will* have different identities, for we as authors have diverse friendships and so likely will our characters. (We strongly urge employing sensitivity readers who share the supporting characters' identities to increase accurate representation.)

#OwnVoices describes a work; it does not describe an author. An author could write one book that is #OwnVoices, and another book that is not. For instance, if a writer from Panama writes about a protagonist that shares one of her marginalized identities, this work would be #OwnVoices. If the same writer from Panama were to write about a protagonist that does not share a marginalized identity, this work would likely not be #OwnVoices. (Keep in mind that "marginalized" identities are relative to the context and audience; Panamanian, for instance, may be a "marginalized" identity relative to a U.S. audience due to global dynamics of oppression and colonization, but may not be marginalized in literature intended for a Panamanian audience.)

#OwnVoices does not mean that an author cannot ever write outside their experience; as Duyvis articulates, "People can write about whatever they want; whether they should is a valid and complex discussion to have — a discussion that's separate from the definition of the term #ownvoices."[55]

We recognize that #OwnVoices has generated some controversy; nonetheless, we believe it is a useful concept for talking about the need for language-learner literature produced by members of target cultures. Please find more more information about the

---

[52] Corinne Duyvis, "#OwnVoices," *Corinne Duyvis: Sci-Fi and Fantasy in MG and YA* [blog], http://www.corinneduyvis.net/ownvoices/ (Accessed 3 July 2020).
[53] Debbie Reese, "Critical Indigenous Literacies: Selecting and Using Children's Books about Indigenous Peoples," *Language Arts* 95.6 (2018), 390.
[54] Duyvis, "#OwnVoices."
[55] Duyvis, ibid.

#OwnVoices movement, including answers to frequently asked questions, in Appendix III to this book.

Since Duyvis conceived the #OwnVoices hashtag and movement to increase literature produced by marginalized cultural voices, and Dr. Reese describes #OwnVoices in the context of cultural voice, this book principally employs the cultural aspect of #OwnVoices. However, our world language field would benefit from further exploration of #OwnVoices with regard to linguistic voice as well.[56]

#OwnVoices is related to similar hashtag movements promoting diversity in North American publishing, such as #DignidadLiteraria, #DiversityJedi, #DisruptTexts and #WeNeedDiverseBooks. Some of these related movements may differ from #OwnVoices in that #OwnVoices emphasizes a shared, marginalized identity between an author and protagonists, whereas the related movement might not emphasize shared identity. Also, some of these related movements focus on a specific cultural group or book genre. We support these hashtag movements and recommend them to readers.

Framework 8: Cultural Styles of Storytelling

Another reason for the importance of #OwnVoices regards the implicit cognitive structures and traditions of storytelling which differ across cultures. When a story about characters in an African, Caribbean or Latin American culture, for instance, is told by a European or North American storyteller, it is almost always subconsciously written through the narrative frameworks of Europe or North America. This framework is embedded in authors often at a subconscious level. #OwnVoices works provide not only a window into the contents and experiences within a culture, but also the very structure of the narrative and cognitive processes common in that culture.

Pakistani American literature professor Dr. Masood Raja explains differing cultural storytelling frameworks:

> The reason I consider [a particular book] an African novel is because it does not try formalistically to be a Western novel. It retains the way of speech, the way of expression, the way of explaining or the way of storytelling that [the author] must have gathered from her own original culture and she kind of represents it. So, the novel doesn't just become a story from [a region of Nigeria], it also becomes an example of the storytelling tradition itself. (3:59-4:40)

---

[56] We as a world language field would benefit from discussion of the application of the #OwnVoices movement not only in its cultural aspect but also its linguistic aspect. Sometimes, so-called "comprehensible" books are written by non-native speakers with unnatural-sounding language that native speakers can barely read. In contrast, however, sometimes non-native speakers write excellent works that native speakers read with pleasure. There is an open discussion waiting about how the concept of #OwnVoices might apply in a linguistic sense to storytelling by writers at different places along their own journey of language proficiency. There is also a conversation waiting to be had about how #OwnVoices applies linguistically when a person from a colonizer country that speaks the TL (such as France or Spain) attempts to represent the linguistic or cultural features from a colonized country that speaks the TL (such as in Africa or Latin America).

> In my graduate classes [at the University of North Texas] I also have creative writing students, and they are taught to write a certain way, which is sort of a Eurocentric way of writing a novel. So I ask them to look at how an African writer sitting in Africa is writing a novel in English, and how is that style different from what is being taught over here [in the United States]. (11:43-12:07)[57]

For the acquisition of a respectful interculturality, students benefit from exposure not only to cultural content and experiences, but also to the metacognitive frameworks that members of a target culture use to process and narrate those experiences. To superimpose a Western storytelling voice on a story ostensibly narrated by an African-, Caribbean- or Latin American-centered storyteller perpetuates, among North American or European readers, the false notion that "everyone else thinks like us." It is a form of imperialism.

Framework 9: Moving beyond binary structures

Binaries in identities: We recognize that personal identities often occupy a fluid space between categories. As such, many people experience interstitial or liminal identities, a sense of "both/and/neither/nor," such as those who (for instance) are second-generation United States residents with roots in a target culture and who identify with a hybrid of multiple cultures.

In order to make specific points in this book, we employ language that can appear to reflect binary, "either/or" categories, such as "member of a target culture" or "non-member of a target culture." As mentioned in the discussion of Framework 1 ("Navigating Sociopolitical Categories"), we acknowledge the limitations of these terms as conceptual tools, as lived realities often transcend the categories afforded to us in language.[58]

We also acknowledge the vast differences *within* social groups, as well as intersectional identities within each individual; as such, it is not possible to *essentialize* members of groups as if binary absolutes like "colonized" or "colonizer" were their essential and only identity. Nonetheless, because social systems of privilege and exclusion do treat individuals in accord with group identities, these labels serve as helpful tools in noticing, analyzing, and responding to patterns of sociological interactions.

Related to *essentialism*, we also reject the notion of *determinism,* as if a past history of marginalization were to prescribe a future reality. "Marginalization" is *descriptive* of social forces of otherization; it is not *prescriptive*. We embrace a paradigm of empowerment that leads to joy-filled liberation and vibrant communities for all--

---

[57] Masood Raja, "Postcolonialism Course (Edited Version), Session 11: *Efuru*: Discussion and Q & A" [Video, 50:21], Postcolonialism [YouTube Channel], https://www.youtube.com/watch?v=OjkJO2FJvjU&list=PLW4ijepGeAnb60jNHo7jxcdBUwSocZUHO&index=18&fbclid=IwAR1Sgy6w-Qya2-uN1_tbuMR-s57WwR3tn7iriiq4-F5yDAT8gQRycCgQQog (accessed 9 February 2021).

[58] As Ludwig Wittgenstein famously asserted, "The limits of my language are the limits of my world."

communities in which notions of *oppressed* and *oppressor* would be a thing of the past--and believe that #OwnVoices language-learner literature plays a key role toward this vision.

Binaries in evaluations: Similarly, we reject the binary notion of "good" and "bad" in discussing books and practices, preferring to see a spectrum of "more/less helpful," "more/less effective," "more/less respectful," practices. This allows us to evaluate professional practices and products with greater nuance, and to position ourselves within a growth mindset as we strive to articulate ideals and to embody them in our work.

Defining Terms and Concepts

The following definitions of terms and concepts are organized by thematic clusters.

TARGET LANGUAGES & TARGET CULTURES

Target Language (TL): The language that we teach, study, or write in.

Target Cultures (TCs): The cultures in which the target language (TL) is widely spoken. Please note: Cultures transcend national borders, as borders are sociopolitical constructions that attempt to divide pre-existing human communities.[59] Consequently, a Peruvian writer, for instance, might be writing about her own community when she writes stories from other Andean regions.

Member of a Target Culture (mTC): This is a person who identifies as belonging to a particular target culture associated with a particular language that is being learned, taught, or written in. This membership is also recognized by other members of that culture.

The acronym "mTC" is a new coinage for this book. The letter 'm' is lowercase to preserve the capitalized 'TC' as an emerging familiar acronym, on par with the very-familiar acronym TL.

mTC is not an abstract and fixed identity, but a situated identity relative to particular cultures. One is a member of particular target cultures and not others. For instance, someone who lives in Chile whose parents are Venezuelan might identify as an mTC of Chile and Venezuela, but this person would likely not also identify as an mTC from another region of Latin America, e.g. Costa Rica.

Someone may be a member of a target culture with regard to an Indigenous group with whom they ancestrally identify, if they are reclaiming their roots. This is more relevant for people from regions in Latin America and the Caribbean that have strong Indigenous

---

[59] The creation of the "nation-state" emerged in 15th-century Europe from efforts to create homogeneous national identities via violent erasure of those communities who did not "fit" with the norms prescribed by ruling powers. As such, we language teachers committed to uncolonization might collectively explore new language for describing target cultures apart from terminology based in nation-states. See Ramón Grosfoguel, "The structure of knowledge in westernized universities: Epistemic racism/sexism and the four genocides/epistemicides," *Human Architecture: Journal of the sociology of self-knowledge* 1 (2013), 79, https://scholarworks.umb.edu/cgi/viewcontent.cgi?article=1445&context=humanarchitecture (accessed 17 July 2020).

ancestral roots than, say, someone from the U.S. who has one Indigenous ancestor from 200 years ago that they found out about from a DNA test.

Some members of target cultures come from *colonizer* cultures, e.g. Spain and France. Other mTCs come from *colonized* cultures, whether *inter*nationally colonized (e.g. Ecuador colonized by Spain; Algeria colonized by France) or *intra*nationally colonized (e.g. Latinx within US). For this book, mTC indicates a member of a *colonized* target culture.

Note: When we discuss membership in a target culture that speaks the target language, we refer to *macrocultures* reflecting regional and/or ethnic identities. We are not referring to microcultures such as our language classrooms, our intentionally multilingual families, or our language-specific clubs, camps or associations. A language teacher could rightly consider themself a member of several such *micro*cultures that speak the target language that they teach, while not being a member of the macrocultures that speak the language.

Non-Members of Target Cultures (nmTC): This is a person who does not identify as a member of a target culture that speaks the language being taught, learned, or written in. The acronym "nmTC" is new coinage for this book.

nmTC is not an abstract and fixed identity, but a situated identity relative to particular cultures that speak a language that one is studying or teaching. For instance, someone who lives in the United States, who is studying Spanish, and who does not have membership in a Latin American country or Latinx community, would be a non-member of target cultures that speak the language he is studying. (If he nonetheless has a close connection to a target culture, see below: "Strong connection to a target culture.")

Referring back to the diagram of Pole A and Pole B in Framework 1 (Navigating Sociopolitical Categories), some non-members of target cultures (Pole B) come from *Imperial/colonizer* cultures (Pole B). Other nmTCs (Pole B) come from *colonized* cultures (Pole A), e.g. a Kenyan teacher of Spanish). As our primary audience is people from Pole B in all three structures of identity in Framework 1, when we say "nmTC" we are primarily envisioning a non-member of a target culture who also belongs to a *Imperial/colonizer* culture.

Strong Connections to a Target Culture: We use this phrase to indicate someone who is a nmTC, but has developed strong and enduring connections to a target culture through adopting a child from that culture, romantic partnership, residency and/or other situations of strong integration into another culture. This is not merely a self-proclaimed strong connection, but one that is recognized as such by members of the target culture. It should be noted, nonetheless, that a strong connection is *not* the same as being a member of a target culture, and does not give one the authority to speak for members of the culture. People with strong connections can erroneously believe that they have such authority, however unconsciously or subconsciously, and end up doing a lot of harm.

Honorary Member of a Target Culture: An honorary member of a target culture goes even deeper than "strong connections" to have *profound connections* to a target culture and be recognized by members of that target culture as one of their own. This would be the case of someone who was born (for instance) in the U.S. but has lived in another culture for decades and has *profoundly* integrated into that culture. For purposes of this book, an honorary member of a target culture might consider themselves a mTC insofar as themes they might represent in literature (although they may still wish to seek the permission of their community before writing).

LITERARY CONCEPTS

Mirrors, Windows, Sliding-Glass Doors, Curtains: See the above section by this name for definitions from Dr. Rudine Sims Bishop and Dr. Debbie Reese.

#OwnVoices: "#OwnVoices is a term coined by the writer Corinne Duyvis, and refers to an author from a marginalized or under-represented group writing about their own experiences/from their own perspective, rather than someone from an outside perspective writing as a character from an underrepresented group." This definition is widely-used on library and bookstore websites; original author unknown. For more discussion, see the discussion in Framework 7 (#OwnVoices) above.

COLONIZATION

Empire: This book makes wide use of the terms "Empire" and "Imperial," and at times uses the term "Empire-identified" to describe an entity (person or system) who has benefitted from being perceived as belonging to the European or North American empires[60] which have oppressed Africans, Asian and Pacific Islanders (API), Indigenous people, Latin Americans and Caribbeans on the American continent, and Black, Indigenous, People of Color in the United States/Canada.

The use of the term "Empire", while it may feel bold and even overly strong to the North American reader, aligns with the perspective of many Latin Americans and Caribbeans, Africans, North American Indigenous, and Asians/Pacific Islanders toward the United States/Canada and Europe. "Empire-identifed" refers to someone who is socially read as belonging to and benefitting from these Imperial powers.

---

[60] Dr. Jonathan Rosa, sociocultural and linguistic anthropologist at Stanford University: "The United States is an empire, but it's not often understood as an imperial, colonial force. ...When you're working within an empire, you need to understand the ways that you're recruited to reproduce the power that is endemic within that empire. ...I would want to struggle with world languages teachers around developing and identifying opportunities for engaging in this kind of a reckoning and thinking about what else is possible." Conlon Perugini, D. (Interviewer), Johnson, S.M. (Producer). (2020). We Teach Languages Episode 142: Language Legitimacy and Imagining New Educational Contexts with Jonathan Rosa [Audio podcast], 33:13-13:54, https://weteachlang.com/2020/06/12/142-with-jonathan-rosa/ (accessed 22 June 2020).

"White" and "Empire-identified" have been generally interchangeable for at least the last 500 years since the European invasion of the Americas[61], as Imperial privileges have been conferred automatically upon White people. However, philosophically speaking, whiteness is "accidental" or external to the essence of the issue: imperialism. Another way of putting it: If you are White, your skin tone is not intrinsically the problem; the problem is the machinations of Empire which attempt to stratify people and that oppress some for the benefit of others such as yourself. For this reason, we refer to *people of whiteness* to indicate that the problem is one of social construction, not biology. People of all skin tones may participate in upholding processes of *whiteness*. See further discussion under the heading "White/people of whiteness" later in this Defining Terms & Concepts section.

"Empire" and "Imperial" are capitalized to indicate the naming of the Western European imperial powers whose legacy now continues in North America. This empire encompasses both North America and Europe.

In this book, we use "Imperial" interchangeably with "colonizer." We acknowledge, as discussed in Frameworks 1 (Navigating Sociopolitical Categories) and 9 (Moving Beyond Binary Structures), that in discussing colonizer and colonized cultures, there are various "in-between" spaces. It is possible to be from both colonizer and colonized identities. For additional reflection, please see the following definitions on international and intranational colonization.

Colonize: To take control of land, property, bodies, religion, ideas and/or cultures belonging to others, without consent, in order to serve the interests of a powerful group; the reinforcement of this control by political, physical and psychological means including the creation of *subalterity*--regarding another as "lesser" (sub) and "other" (alter).

Colonizer: See "Empire."

Colonized: Communities at the receiving end of colonization, both historically and currently. This term is most common in discourse pertaining to Latin America and the Caribbean, Africa and parts of Asia. We are fans of the word "colonized" in that it names historic and current realities[62] so that they can lead to *conscientización*--an awakening

---

[61] The social construct of race emerged alongside the colonial expansion of Empire in the Americas. Puerto Rican sociologist Ramón Grosfoguel comments, "State racism is not a post-18th century phenome- non, but a phenomenon that emerged following the conquest of the Americas in the 16th century." See Grosfoguel, "The structure of knowledge in westernized universities: Epistemic racism/sexism and the four genocides/epistemicides," *Human Architecture: Journal of the sociology of self-knowledge* 1 (2013), 82, https://scholarworks.umb.edu/cgi/viewcontent.cgi?article=1445&context=humanarchitecture (accessed 17 July 2020).

[62] Naming realities can be perceived as divisive, but is necessarily for dealing with issues. As author Laurie Olsen comments, "To raise concerns about the lack of access or the problems in teaching is difficult. To name inequality is believed to be impolite at best, divisive in most contexts" (26). The inequalities and their roots need to be named. See Olsen, *Made in America: Immigrant Students in Our Public Schools* (New York: The New Press, 2008).

about social dynamics that leads to resistance and change. We are not big fans of the word "colonized" to describe people insofar as it implies being *acted upon,* in contrast with *having agency.* In response to this conundrum, we have used "colonized" in reference to regions and communities, not specific people. Our preference would be to replace "colonized" insofar as it refers to communities with a term implying collective agency and resilience, such as *Pueblo*,[63] the people. However, for practical reasons, we use "colonized."

International colonization: This refers to processes of colonization and oppression that occur *between* nations on an international level, for example, the colonization of Latin America and the Caribbean, Africa, and Asia (in part) by Great Britain, France, and Spain. This colonization continues in the current day by not only European powers but also their heirs such as the United States, Canada, Australia and South Africa.

Intranational colonization: This refers to processes of colonization and oppression that occur *within* nations, for example, dominant powers in the U.S. creating "subaltern" (so-called *lesser* and *other*) classes of various communities of color; elite classes in Latin America creating subaltern classes of Indigenous communities within their country; etc.

Uncolonize: The acts of detaching from, divesting from, and dismantling processes of colonialism, by those who are not Indigenous.

"Uncolonize" is distinct from the term "decolonize," which refers to Indigenous movements for the return of land, leadership and resources to Indigenous control. Many Indigenous communities assert that "decolonization is not a metaphor" but refers to the concrete rematriation/repatriation described above.[64] We are responding to leadership

---

[63] This preference is inspired by the words of Argentinean writer Enrique Angelelli in the early 1970s, *"Pueblo es el que no oprime y lucha contra la opresión... El antipueblo es la fuerza que responde a intereses extraños. Está personificado en una minoría que quiere conservar sus privilegios. Es el que impide el crecimiento del pueblo y lucha por hundirlo en la opresión y en la esclavitud. Es el que frena nuestra historia. Es el que entrega inescrupulosamente nuestro patrimonio posibilitando una dependencia económica de grandes intereses internacionales."* Pueblo is the group that doesn't oppress and that struggles against oppression… The anti-Pueblo is the force that responds to foreign interests. It's personified in the minority that wants to preserve its privileges. It's the group that impedes the growth of the Pueblo and actively works toward drowning it in oppression and slavery. It's the group that puts the breaks on our history. It's the group that unscrupulously gives away what belongs to us, making possible an economic dependency on huge international interests (Translation K. Lentz with A. Ramírez). Enrique Angelelli, quoted in Unidad Popular Santa Fe, "Hay Que Seguir Andando Nomás," https://unidadpopular santafe.org/2016/08/01/hay-que-seguir-andando-nomas/ (accessed 20 July 2020).

[64] See Eve Tuck and K. Wayne Yang who, in their 2012 essay "Decolonization is not a metaphor," have pointed out that "Decolonization brings about the repatriation of Indigenous land and life; it is not a metaphor for other things we want to do to improve our societies and schools." Tuck and Yang, "Decolonization is not a metaphor," *Decolonization: Indigeneity, Education & Society* (Vol. 1, No. 1, 2012), 1, https://clas.osu.edu/sites/clas.osu.edu/files/Tuck%20and%20Yang%202012%20Decolonization%20is%20not%20a%20metaphor.pdf (accessed 25 March 2021).

from Indigenous communities[65] in our context of the United States and Canada about the use of these terms, while cognizant that their use will likely be different in other parts of the world where colonization has historically played out very differently than in North America.

Country names: At some places in this book, we refer to countries by name. We want to acknowledge the artificiality of national borders and national names, as both were imposed by colonial powers to serve their own interests.[66] In this book, when we refer to countries by name, it is for clarity of communication. We recommend maps such as the crowd-sourced Native Land map (native-land.ca) and the continental maps[67] at Indigenous Peoples Resources (indigenouspeoplesresources.com) for an uncolonized representation of regional place names and tribal nations.

MORE ON IDENTITIES

Note: We acknowledge that these are broad terms and none of these groups are monoliths.

Latin American, Caribbean and Latinx: We use these terms broadly to refer to people who identify as members of communities with origins in South America, Central America, the Caribbean and Mexico (including historic Mexico prior to the 1848 transfer to the United States), regardless of current location of residence.

For the purposes of this book, *Latin American/Caribbean* and *Latinx* are used interchangeably. This is not to overlook the distinctions, but to indicate commonality of historic oppression by the Empire among communities whose members identify with one or more of these often-overlapping identities.

We acknowledge that *Latin-* is a naming system based in colonization and use it as interim nomenclature until uncolonized naming practices become widely indicated as preferred terms.

---

[65] See Tanya Rodriguez, "Decolonization, A Guide for Settlers Living on Stolen Land," *Tanya Rodriguez* [blog], 26 December 2020, https://gdiriseup.medium.com/decolonization-a-guidebook-for-settlers-living-on-stolen-land-57d4e4c04bbb (accessed 15 April 2021).

[66] Côte d'Ivoire-based reggae artist Tiken Jah Fakoly sings about the history of Empire-imposed borders in Africa in the song "Plus rien ne m'étonne": Ils ont partagé le monde, plus rien ne m'étonne / Ils ont partagé Africa sans nous consulter / Ils s'étonnent que nous soyons désunis ! / Une partie de l'empire Mandingue / Se trouva chez les Wolofs / Une partie de l'empire Mossi / Se trouva dans le Ghana ... *(They shared the world, nothing surprises me anymore / They shared Africa without consulting us / They are surprised that we are disunited! / Part of the Mandingo Empire / Was among the Wolofs / Part of the Mossi Empire / Was in Ghana ...)* Fakoly, "Plus rien ne m'étonne", track 1 on *Coup de guele*, Barclay Records, 2004. English translation courtesy of Google Translate, https://g.co/kgs/RVZbhQ (accessed 7 March 2021).

[67] We advise caution regarding maps that unintentionally reify colonial boundaries, such as maps limited to the current shape of the United States. We recommended seeking out the maps that transcend colonially-imposed borders to show Indigenous tribal nations across continents or regions.

Latinx is used for gender inclusivity in the English-language context of this work. It could alternatively read as *Latina, Latino* or *Latine*, depending on the preferences of the individual or community to whom it refers.

African: We use this term broadly to refer to all people who identify as members of African communities or as members of African diasporas, regardless of current location of residence.

Asian-Pacific Islander (API): We use this term broadly to refer to all people who identify as members of Asian-Pacific Islander communities or as members of API diasporas, regardless of current location of residence.

European: We use this term broadly to refer to all people who identify as members of European communities or as members of European diasporas, regardless of current location of residence. "European" includes countries of the former European empires that continue its imperial legacy, such as Australia and South Africa. While "European" generally connotes power, we acknowledge the presence of marginalized groups both currently and historically in Europe.

North American: Specifically the United States and Canada. While Mexico is part of North America, this book addresses North American imperial powers.

Native-speaker: For the purposes of this book, when we refer to a *native-speaker* we mean someone who speaks a language as their first language or a language since early childhood. For practical purposes, we are including in this category people who identify as *heritage speakers*--someone whose elder relatives spoke a language with them, but who may themselves have varying levels of proficiency.

You refers to the primary intended audience of this book as defined in Framework 1 ("Navigating Sociopolitical Categories").

Black, Indigenous, People of Color (BIPOC): People who identify as having an identity of Black, Brown, Indigenous, Asian-Pacific Islander, and/or other groups historically otherized by the construction of White identity.

Long-time Black activist Loretta Ross explains that the term "people of color" transcends ethnic or biological identity to encompass a political definition: "It is a solidarity definition, a commitment to work in collaboration with other oppressed [people] of color who have been minoritized. … When you choose to work with other people who are minoritized by oppression you have lifted yourself out of that basic [ethnic] identity into another political being, another political space. Unfortunately so many times people of color hear the term people of color from other white people that they think white people created it instead of understanding that we self-named ourselves; this is a term that has a lot of power for us."[68]

White/people of whiteness: When using language of racialization, we refer interchangeably in this book to *White* and to *people of whiteness*. The National Museum of African American History and Culture observes that "Whiteness and white racialized identity refer to the way that white people, their customs, culture, and beliefs operate as the standard by which all other groups are compared."[69] The construction of whiteness is closely tied to the construction of Imperial power.

Whiteness / White racialized identity, like all racialized identities, is a social construction and not a biological reality.[70] However, people socially-read as White accrue privileges and power in a system of White supremacy and Imperial power, and often uphold that system with or without explicit consciousness of it. In addition, some people who are *not* socially-read as White also participate in upholding processes of whiteness, White supremacy and Imperial power.

A note on style: There is a debate in contemporary literature and journalism about the choice of whether to capitalize racialized terms such as *Black, Brown, White*. This book follows the most current style guidelines for bias-free language from the American Psychological Association (APA), which indicate capitalized usage for racialized identities.[71] As the APA uses lowercase for *people of color,* for consistency we also use lowercase for *people of whiteness*. The exception is when writing out "Black, Indigenous, People of Color," in which case *People of Color* is capitalized for consistency with *Black* and *Indigenous*.

WORLD LANGUAGE PROFESSION

Simplified/Sheltered/Comprehensible Input: *Comprehensible input* involves repetition of high-frequency vocabulary and structures for language acquisition, and heavy use of

---

[68] Loretta Ross, "The origin of the term 'women of color'" [interview], Western States Center, 28 January 2011, https://www.youtube.com/watch?v=82vl34mi4lw (accessed 18 January 2021).

[69] National Museum of African American History and Culture, "Talking About Race: Whiteness," undated, https://nmaahc.si.edu/learn/talking-about-race/topics/whiteness (accessed 28 November 2020). This excellent resource contains interactive and multimedia educational resources about whiteness from Robin diAngelo, bell hooks, Peggy McIntosh, and others.

[70] For a helpful resource, see Kay Young McChesney, "Teaching Diversity: The Science You Need to Know to Explain Why Race Is Not Biological," SAGE Open, 16 October 2015, https://journals.sagepub.com/doi/10.1177/2158244015611712 (accessed 28 November 2020).

[71] American Psychological Association, "Racial and Ethnic Identity," 2020, https://apastyle.apa.org/style-grammar-guidelines/bias-free-language/racial-ethnic-minorities (accessed 22 October 2020). Interestingly, different writing style guides currently take different approaches to capitalization of racialized identities. The Associated Press, as of July 2020, advocates using uppercase for Black and lowercase for White. The Chicago/Turabian style--the style manual for most of this book--as of July 2020 advocates a more flexible, context-dependent approach to capitalization. Out of a desire for consistency in style with regard to capitalization, we have chosen the APA as a guide for this aspect of style in this book. It will be interesting to see how style guides evolve over time in this regard.

cognates, as part of the process of *simplifying* and *sheltering* language in order to facilitate language acquisition. These processes are utilized by language education professionals across a wide umbrella of methodologies. Although professionals in the field discuss differences in these terms, in order to reach the widest possible audience, we refer interchangeably to language-learner literature as "comprehensible," "simplified" and/or "sheltered."

WL: World Language, referring to the profession of world language education.

Author: This includes authors of novels, short stories and other reading materials, including curriculum, for language learners in the world language (WL) field.

Teacher: This refers to teachers in the world language (WL) profession.

Language-Learners (LLs): People who are learning another language in addition to their first language.

Language-learner literature: This is literature written for language learners, typically employing sheltered vocabulary, cognates and multiple repetitions of high-frequency words to increase comprehensibility for the goal of language acquisition. While it is intended for learners of a new language, ideally it is written in such a way that native speakers may enjoy the literature as well, particularly people learning how to read who can benefit from simplified texts.

Spanish and French: The document refers to Spanish and French as they are the most frequently-taught languages other than English in the United States. Teachers of other languages may replace references to Spanish and French with a reference to the language they teach. The same goes for teachers replacing a mention of the regions where French and Spanish are spoken (e.g. Africa, the Caribbean, Latin America) with the countries or regions where the language they teach is spoken, particularly if that culture has experienced oppression at the hands of an Imperial power.

BOOK PRODUCTION

Cultural Consultants: This refers to members of target cultures who have first-hand knowledge and expertise about their target cultures' products, practices, and perspectives. Cultural consultants unfinished manuscripts with the specific purpose of ensuring accurate description of such products, practices, and perspectives. *Important note:* A cultural consultant may have expertise in cultural products, practices, and perspectives but may not have the experience/skills necessary to be a sensitivity reader (see below).

Sensitivity Readers: This refers to individuals who are skilled in reading an unpublished manuscript specifically for the purpose of finding misrepresentations, bias, stereotypes, and any other problematic language or narratives. It is helpful to have sensitivity readers who can look at texts for a wide variety of intersectional issues: ableism, racialization, classism, gender and sexuality justice, etc.

CULTURE

Deep culture: Elements of a culture that are more implicit. Some teachers refer to this as "Little C" culture. Please refer to the description from Zaretta Hammond in Framework 4 ("Stories that 'belong' to others/Deep culture").

Surface culture: Elements of culture that are readily observable from the outside. Some teachers refer to this as "Big C" culture. Please see Framework 4 ("Stories that "Belong" to Others + The Problems We Perpetuate") for a discussion of how surface elements in stories also 'belong' to a culture.

Higher-cultural-embeddedness: This refers to the extent to which a book's themes and plot are enmeshed inextricably from the cultural setting.

Lower-cultural-embeddedness: This refers to the extent to which a book's themes and plot are somewhat extricable from their cultural setting and could be transferred to another setting without causing major alteration to the themes or plot.

PART THREE: ACTION

ACTION is the third stage of the observe-analyze-act cycle of social action/praxis.

.....

This section discusses the proposed paths for writing toward the acquisition of respectful interculturality. It begins with a preface about cultural consultants and sensitivity readers, followed by an overview of the paths, and then details action plans for Paths A-D. This section concludes with questions and answers, a summary, and closing words.

.....

PREFACE: Cultural Consultants and Sensitivity Readers

Cultural Consultants and Sensitivity Readers are important in each of the action paths presented below. Compensate them[72] for their time and effort, and acknowledge their contributions to your work, perhaps even including a forward from them saying they approve of the work. It is helpful to engage their participation at multiple stages of the creative process, for efficiency. (It is painful to undo many hours of work for something that could have been prevented had their involvement occurred earlier!) The following describes each role:

Cultural Consultants: If a story involves a (sub)culture that is not shared by the author/s, then cultural consultants need to be involved in preparing the manuscript. This applies for characters and settings.

> A **cultural consultant** is someone who...
> ...is a member of the culture(s) represented in a manuscript.
> ...has first-hand knowledge and expertise about their culture's products, practices, and perspectives.
> ...reads unfinished manuscripts with the specific purpose of ensuring accurate descriptions and illustrations of products, practices, and perspectives.

---

[72] Since many writers are teachers on a low budget, the compensation aspect can be a challenge. Keep in mind that compensation can take various forms, including products or an exchange of services.

> ...<u>will not</u> simply say "yes" to you because of your membership in groups and identities that are generally considered or perceived to be powerful.

A cultural consultant, despite their expertise in cultural products, practices, and perspectives, may or may not have the experience/skills necessary to also be a sensitivity reader. Sometimes you will get lucky and have a cultural consultant who also has the skill set of a sensitivity reader. However, these are different roles and typically are played by different people.

When authors falsely assume that the cultural consultant is also a sensitivity reader, they end up publishing a text with a lot of problems to clean up afterward. These problems include:
- hurting students (and even though they are unlikely to tell the author or teacher that they are hurt, or even to realize it, at a subconscious level they still see it)[73]
- impeding social justice and equality by perpetuating racist or ethnocentrist myths
- hurting the very people with whom they attempt to build intercultural bridges
- the costs of republishing
- public backlash on social media
- loss of credibility
- putting teachers in a very difficult position of complicity with oppression when they put this book on their free voluntary reading libraries without the chance to address these aspects in conversation with students[74]

Again, to reiterate: Just because a cultural consultant is from the target culture doesn't mean they have the ultimate word on the extent to which something is acceptable. Also, employ sensitivity readers, ideally some from both the target culture and some from the culture of the intended audience.

Sensitivity Readers offer essential collaboration because most of us do not see all of the implicit biases we unwittingly can perpetuate.[75]

---

[73] Education librarian Edith Campbell: "Educators and librarians can't afford the privilege of [not noticing biases] with regard to picture books, particularly if they're striving to educate young people in an atmosphere of equality and social justice. Those who produce books, teach children, or work in libraries need training to consciously push past their own biases so that they don't perpetuate anti-Blackness myths." In Edith Campbell, "The Problem with Picture Book Monkeys: Racist imagery associating simians with Black people has a long history," *School Library Journal,* 4 December 2019, https://www.slj.com/The-problem-with-picture-book-monkeys-racist-imagery-libraries (accessed 9 July 2020).

[74] "If we're reading these books to children or are placing them on shelves, we're complicit in the racism they promote unless we actively engage with the text through a lens of critical literacy addressing the representations of power." -- Campbell, ibid.

[75] "In the majority-White world of children's publishing, many people are still unaware of their own implicit bias. So when racist images are unwittingly created by one person or department, others may not see it." -- Campbell, ibid.

A **sensitivity reader** is someone who…
…has skills to read an unpublished manuscript specifically for the purpose of finding misrepresentations, bias, stereotypes, generalization, essentializing, and any other problematic language or narratives.
…is not necessarily an educator (although this is helpful as we educators tend to see things with other eyes, thanks to our students).
…is awake to disrupting dynamics of oppression and colonization.
…<u>will</u> give you critical, non-sugar-coated feedback.

It is helpful to have a team of sensitivity readers who can look at texts for a wide variety of intersectional issues: ableism; racialization; classism; gender and sexuality justice; neurodiversity; religion; intercultural racialization and paternalism; etc. Keep in mind that different sensitivity readers may be best-positioned to read for different issues; a person with keen eyes for classism, for instance, may or may not have the same sharp lenses for ableism. This is why a team of sensitivity readers is essential.

As oppression often manifests differently in various cultural contexts, it helps to employ sensitivity readers both from the culture(s) of the intended audience as well as from the culture(s) being portrayed in the manuscript through the characters and the settings.

Like cultural consultants, it is ideal to involve sensitivity readers at multiple stages of the writing process.

WRITING ALONG THE PATHS: OVERVIEW CHART

Paths for non-members of target cultures to contribute to the creation of new language-learner literature that honors the principles of #OwnVoices

The following chart provides an overview of models for non-members of target cultures to contribute to the creation of new reading material for world language learners. It is not an exhaustive list, nor are the models mutually exclusive; instead, it is intended to open potentially new vistas to inform our collective professional conversation. The path one chooses depends principally on whether the theme of the writing project involves representation of a target culture (Path A vs. Paths B/C/D); considerations about extent of authorial engagement (Paths A/B/C vs. Path D); and the author's desire for recognition (Paths A/B vs. Paths C/D).

On the pages following this chart, please find extended descriptions of each model.

Content Theme: Non-Target Cultures

Path A: Writing Stories from Your Own (Sub)Cultures

Write stories in the target language using your own voice, from the perspective of your (or your community's) own unique subculture and experiences. Your story is not attempting to represent someone else's culture/s but to provide a window to your own, and to hold up a mirror to the students who share your (sub)culture/s. In this path, it may also be possible to produce your own #OwnVoices literature if you are writing from a marginalized identity you share with your protagonist.

Content Theme: Target Cultures

For WL Authors (including curriculum writers)		For WL Teachers, Authors and Others
Path B: Collaborating	**Path C: Facilitating**	**Path D: Scribing**
For WL authors who seek… … to collaborate with voices from target cultures … creative authorial engagement … a finished product in their name	For WL authors who seek… … to use their skill set as a consultant with new authors from the target cultures … to serve behind the scenes	For WL teachers, authors and others who seek… …to assist members of the TL and TC in giving birth to their own stories … to serve behind the scenes
Model B-1: Parallel Thematic Stories (nmTC and mTC authors each making a distinct work from their own subjective perspective, connected to each other) **Model B-2: Interwoven-Voices Book** (nmTC and mTC authors each contributing different chapters from their subjective perspective) **Model B-3: Co-writing** (nmTC and mTC authors crafting the same text) **Model B-4: Adaptation** (nmTC author adapts a published text for language learners) **Model B-5: Co-production of a Graphic Novel** (nmTC and mTC authors collaborate on a graphic novel)	**Model C-1: Ghostwriting** (nmTC author crafts mTC's story from behind the scenes while the mTC gets authorial credit) **Model C-2: Recruit New Voices and Serve as Consultant** (nmTC author uses their skills to equip a new mTC author to create a story)	**Scribing (Language Experience Approach / Dictated Stories)** (mTC storyteller dictates their story to an nmTC scribe; the mTC storyteller might later choose Model B-4 or C-2 for the adaptation of their story for language-learners)

PATH A

WRITING STORIES FROM YOUR OWN (SUB)CULTURES

> OVERVIEW: Write stories in the target language using your own voice, from the perspective of yourself or your community's own unique subculture and experiences. Your story is not attempting to represent someone else's culture but to provide a window to your own, and to hold up a mirror to the students who share your (sub)culture/s. In this path, it may also be possible to produce your own #OwnVoices literature if you are writing from a marginalized identity you share with your protagonist.

Non-members of target culture (nmTC) authors: You have a powerful voice. Use it! In the Target Language!

Write stories about all sorts of stuff from *your own culture, subcultures, and experiences!* It's okay to write stories set in your own geographic location. Language students and teachers really need stories from a wide variety of *subcultures* in North American and European regions. We as teachers need windows into the subcultures our students inhabit, and mirrors in which they can see themselves. nmTC authors have an extremely important role of providing classrooms with materials that represent the wide variety of subcultures represented by students and teachers in the language-learning community.

Contrary to what some nmTC authors may fear at first, mTC authors are *not* trying to tell nmTC authors not to write; rather, they are trying to protect the stories of their cultures, while urging nmTC teachers to author stories in target languages with the voice that they *do* have.

You don't have to choose between writing insulated North American or European stories or "cultural" stories from other countries. The United States, for instance, as a very intercultural and multilingual nation, has its own compelling stories. If you are BIPOC, you might write from your context, in the TL, giving students stories with which to identify and which promote empowerment. If you are White, you might write stories showing students how to be an effective ally and accomplice in current social issues.

If you find yourself drawn to stories that highlight people helping others, then instead of having characters go volunteer in TC communities (thus perpetuating White saviorist mentalities), consider focusing on how your characters engage deeply with social action in their home communities.[76]

Consider the many settings in North America that model opportunities for intercultural communication across subcultures, for example, a North American public middle school where social divisions form around the economic class of the elementary school one attended. Settings such as these provide an opportunity to demonstrate characters deconstructing stereotypes, breaking down lines of us-them, unlearning prejudices and growing in empathy: all goals of intercultural communication within the microcosm of inter-subcultural settings, skills which lay the groundwork for intercultural communication across broader cultural differences.

Also consider writing from the many target-language microcultures of which you may be a member as a language teacher. Some examples might include: your language classroom; multilingual family home life; and any language-specific clubs, camps and associations.

Deconstruct this notion that Spanish, French and other target languages are the languages of "other countries." The territories named by colonizers as the United States and Canada are very multilingual countries. You can write stories from these places. In the context of the United States, for instance, there could be French stories set in the area now known as Louisiana; Japanese stories set in the West Coast; Arabic stories set in the Great Lakes area; German stories set in the midwest; etc.[77] It would be especially powerful for authors to write stories showing the relatively lengthy histories of many world languages in North America, while keeping in mind for readers that all non-Indigenous languages are newcomers to this continent. Of course, if you are not a

---

[76] This local social action sets the stage for later international solidarity work--and some great **Path B** novel sets--in which people eventually do travel to another culture, not to "help" or "save" people in that culture, but to engage in mutual strategizing about how to address issues that are similarly encountered in both the host culture and the home culture. This kind of international solidarity relies on a prerequisite deep engagement with social action in one's local context. For an example, see the work of Witness for Peace / Solidarity Collective, which brings together North American and Latin American/Caribbean community organizers for collaboration and inspiration on issues occurring in both their respective home contexts.

[77] We don't mention here the writing of Indigenous language stories set in different places of the land currently called the United States because this book is directed to authors/teachers who are *not* members of target cultures that speak the target language, and we are assuming that teachers/writers of indigenous languages *are* cultural insiders to that language.

member of one of those communities, either ancestrally or currently, then a story representing that community is not your story to tell, even if based in the United States/Canada.

Write lesser-told stories about the history of our own nations. Inspired by books like Howard Zinn and Rebecca Stefoff's *A Young People's History of the United States*,[78] author the histories that are often not included in traditional curriculum, as long as the stories are yours to tell. If not, please refer to Paths B, C, D.

Consider writing from the intersections of your own identity. What are your personal experiences that you can bring to a story? What things can you share that will help your students to know that they are not "the only one" going through an experience? We need to bring to the fore these subcultural issues that transcend various geographic locations, as experienced through our own subcultural lenses.

    Some examples of writing from one's own identity:
    - A.C. Quintero: *La clase de confesiones* (a Black high school student in love)
    - Cécile Lainé: *Camille* (a White French dancer teen with a curvy body)
    - Carol Gaab: *Brandon Brown wants a dog* (a White U.S. child who wants a dog)

In thinking about writing from the intersections of our own identities, we are sometimes faced with a challenge: If we write about a protagonist who shares one of our marginalized and concealed identities, are we then forced to "out" that identity? The creator of the #OwnVoices hashtag, Corinne Duyvis, responds to this question: "Nobody is under any obligation to disclose any part of their identity. Safety and privacy are essential."[79] The issue still remains, though, about how an author might respond if they are accused of appropriating a marginalized voice that they privately share. However, it lies outside the scope of this book as we are specifically addressing #OwnVoices as it relates to generally public identities such as membership in target cultures that speak the target languages we teach. We recommend reading more about Duyvis' reflections on #OwnVoices in Appendix III of this book and continually engaging in our world language community with the discussions happening within the broader #OwnVoices movement.

It's helpful to preface your work with a "social location" statement. By letting your readers know where you are writing from, both geographically and with regard to your relevant identities, it helps them to understand how to interpret the authenticity of the perspectives in the work. Keep in mind, as discussed above, that any social location statement is based on the personal information that you wish to disclose. It is also helpful

---

[78] Howard Zinn with Rebecca Stefoff, *A Young People's History of the United States: Columbus to the War on Terror* (New York: Penguin Random House, 2001).
[79] Corinne Duyvis, "#OwnVoices," http://www.corinneduyvis.net/ownvoices/ (accessed 10 July 2020).

to be transparent about the contributions of communities who helped you to understand the perspectives of various characters in the book.

Consider also focusing on the challenges and joys of ordinary life. Take care not to create "issues-only" books--does a book with an neurodivergent protagonist, for instance, have to feature ADHD or autism or dyslexia as the central plot? (No!)[80] Create protagonists of a variety of different identities demonstrating agency, joy and resilience in everyday situations. These books serve as mirrors and windows to our students.

Our classroom free-voluntary-reading libraries need to be filled with books to target the interests of *all students* so that they can fall in love with reading. We need books that reflect a wide variety of student interests: clarinet, soccer, friends, crushes, gender identity, summer break, the environment, etc. These can be #OwnVoices books from target cultures, or books from non-target cultures. We want them to read independently and fall in love with reading by seeing themselves in the novels they read.[81] A good example of this is A.C. Quintero's book of realistic fiction, *La Clase de Confesiones*--students often chuckle while reading because they can see themselves in the plot! Let's fill libraries with many more such "mirrors" by which students may see their lives reflected in their independent reading, and "windows" by which their peers can come to know them better.

#OwnVoices in Path A: While the focus of this project is increasing the amount of #OwnVoices language-learner literature from target cultures, keep in mind that if you write in Path A about protagonists from your context who share a marginalized aspect of identity with you, you will be producing highly-sought-after #OwnVoices literature to empower students of various identities (e.g. race, ethnicity, disability status, LGBTQIA+, neurodivergence, economic class, etc.).

---

[80] Novelist Rachael Lucas: "I'm really sick of novels by people not on the spectrum telling us how it feels to be autistic and using autistic characters as props to make a sentimental point. Whereas in fact, we're just out here getting on with living our lives. I wanted to write a book in which the character was autistic but that wasn't the point of the story. It was a coming of age. Will she find a boyfriend? How's she getting on with her friends? The things all young girls go through. She just happens to be autistic." In Laura James, *Odd Girl Out: My Extraordinary Autistic Life* (Berkeley, CA: Seal, 2018), 229.

[81] Psychologist Jacques Lacan talks about the building of our own identities with what we see reflected on the outside world. Lacan explains that we build our identities when we are small children, but that this process does not end there; it continues shaping us throughout our lives, especially in adolescence. He talks about the power of physical mirrors in the process of recognizing ourselves and saying, "That is me." This is a very powerful psychological process that shapes our understanding of who we are.

Building on Lacan, we can take this further with applications to literature: Those mirrors are also stories; they don't have to be physical mirrors, but narrative mirrors that help us see ourselves reflected in the outside world. Therefore, these mirrors form an important part in our ever-constant process of building and re-building our identities. When we see ourselves reflected in the stories we read and in the people who write them, we have the same powerful process of identification: we say "That is me," which shapes who we are and how we self-identify.

Variants on Path A:

- Path A could be done collaboratively with other nmTC authors. It might be especially interesting for two nmTC authors from different (sub)cultures—perhaps one from an Empire-identified context, one from a colonized context--to collaborate on a book within the general parameters of Path A, using the collaborative structures proposed in Path B. This collaboration could yield some fascinating writing projects: a non-Latinx Canadian and a non-Latinx Kenyan, for instance, writing in Spanish about shared themes in their own contexts.

- Path A is also a way to generate classroom material from nmTC students and community voices. You might also invite students and other storytellers and authors from the Empire-identified culture to generate language-learner literature from their own subcultural perspectives (parallel to Paths C or D for inviting mTC-authored material), with authorial attributions, of course, given to the storytellers and authors.

PATH B: COLLABORATING

OVERVIEW: In Path B, the content theme includes target cultures. Authors who are not members of target cultures collaborate with authors from target cultures. Both/all authors engage creatively. Both/all authors create works in their names.

------------------------ MODEL B-1 ------------------------

MODEL B-1: PAIRED THEMATIC BOOKS. An authorial duo -- one identified with an Empire-identified culture, one identified with a target culture (TC) -- agrees to each write a book at the same language-acquisition level (e.g. Novice-High) on a similar theme. This allows for genuine work with the Comparisons strand of the 5 Cs. For instance: fair trade apples in Washington State in the U.S., and fair trade coffee in Ecuador. Each writer writes from their own context. Care must be taken that decision-making on theme and language level occurs jointly, and we recommend that preference in decision-making be given to the TC writer to offset the power that frequently gets granted, even subconsciously, to Empire-identified authors.

Ideally, the author duo will also publish their paired books in the language of the other so that language learners in both of their regions can read and compare cultural ways of interacting with a common theme. This builds solidarity and mutual collaboration around global issues. For example, the apples book and the coffee book could both be published in Spanish and in English, for the benefit of language learners in both languages.

Examples of paired common themes	
New Year's Eve in New York City (U.S.)	New Year's Eve in Caracas, Venezuela
Fair-trade apples in Washington State (U.S.)	Fair-trade coffee in Ecuador
My grandpa the miner in Kentucky (U.S.)	A miner in Guatemala
(Book written from the perspective of a nmTC author)	(Book written from the #OwnVoices perspective of a mTC author)

Additional Notes on Model B-1 (Paired Thematic Voices):
- In addition to use in world language programs, these paired thematic books could also be extremely beneficial for ELL students to have cross-cultural book sets in both their home language and new language. They would also benefit cross-continental / cross-cultural curriculum development.
- As in any other collaborative relationship, the author duo will experience mutual vulnerability in their work together.
- The diagram above includes stories of mining, which has historically been fraught with labor abuse issues. Choose themes with care if a paired-book set is likely the students' first point of entry into a culture. It would be wise for an author duo to do not just one pair of books, but a *series* of paired books together, to introduce students to a culture with lighter topics, then to increase in seriousness as the students come to know the variegated nature of both cultures.

------------------------ **MODEL B-2** ------------------------

MODEL B-2: INTERWOVEN VOICES IN A SINGLE BOOK: An authorial duo--one from Empire, one from a colonized target culture--agree to collaborate on *a single book* that weaves two voices, with each voice speaking in its own section or chapter. This requires very close collaboration. This could be a pen pal book as exemplified by Paula Danziger and Ann M. Martin in the children's novel *P.S. Longer Letter Later;* or a book from multiple voices, such as the films *Crash* or *Babel* which have multiple voices converging on a single theme; or any other combinations--the sky's the limit.

For example, an Alaskan and a Panamanian writer might collaborate on a school-based story, perhaps as Skype pen pals. Students can see the differences between both places and how this affects daily lives. It is essential, in doing this writing, to stress that NO culture should be essentialized into a single story, or fetishized as if it is "so cool" when it is really just normal life for the people living it.

Deeper political topics can also be approached.[82] For instance, a Chilean and U.S. writer might collaborate on a story set in September 1973. What were they each doing when the United States caused a coup d'état in Chile, without most U.S. residents knowing anything about it? Or a story set in September 2001. What were they each doing when the United States went through its own 9/11?

Stories might center around a single date in time, or a single worldwide phenomenon as seen from different angles.

If difficult or traumatic topics are chosen, this must be with the <u>consent</u> and <u>desire</u> of the writer whose culture is most deeply affected by the trauma. Also, carefully consider the purpose. Is it to titillate the reader with fear, shock, etc.--thus exploiting the trauma? Or, for situations such as the events of 9/11/73, is the purpose to educate the reader on the reality of United States intervention, with the goal of mobilizing resistance to present-day imperialism? This would depend upon <u>the wishes of the Chilean writer</u> and their community of accountability, and whether or not they want for a new generation of U.S. students to know their story. They are in control of *when, how,* and *if* it's told.

Another model might be for the two authors to write from voices of two people in a single geographic location. For instance, an exchange student from Canada and her Costa Rican host sister could each tell parts of a story in their own voice. This would be

---

[82] In an earlier generation, authors of language-learner material were told to avoid political hot topics; however, many districts are now open to politicized content. Of course, staying silent on important topics was a political act in and of itself. And, as the famous refrain goes, "the personal is political." However, we now have the stamp of approval, in many districts, to create this explicitly more controversial material without as much fear that districts and teachers will not select it for classroom use. For example, see the "Guidelines for Positive Non-Stereotyped Portrayal of Human Roles in Curriculum Materials" from Des Moines School District in Iowa. http://www.dmschools.org/wpcontent/uploads/2011/10/AP-Biology-.pdf (Thanks to Karen Rowan in her "How to Write a CI Novel" workshop, Spring 2020, for sharing this resource.)

like the *Pobre Ana*[83] genre of intercultural exchange, re-spun in two voices. Or perhaps a book might feature a new student in a U.S. school and her classmate(s). The reader then gets to compare the interior monologue of each person, through the cultural perspective of each.

Important: Each protagonist is portrayed *through the lens and voice of someone from that person's culture.* Decision-making power is shared between the authors, with preference given to the colonized-target-culture writer (as discnitsed for **Model B-1**).

This calls for a very strong level of interdependence and collaboration between the authors.

> Single novel with 2+ authors
>
> Perspectives from 2+ different cultures (mTC and nmTC), with each voice residing in its own separate section

---

[83] *Pobre Ana:* A classic language-learner novel involving a U.S. American girl who travels to Mexico and has intercultural exchanges. Blaine Ray, *Pobre Ana: Una novela breve y fácil totalmente en español,* ed. Contee Seely (Berkeley, CA: Command Performance Language Institute, 2000).

MODEL B-3

MODEL B-3: COWRITING. With co-writing, 2+ authors craft the same text. They are not each crafting their own chapter or section, as in **Model B-2** (Interwoven Voices) but both working on the same text on a micro level. This requires extremely close collaboration. It might involve authors crafting the dialogue of the protagonists from their culture. It might even involve collaboration on the same sentences. We leave it up to the readers to imagine how this model might work. We advise many of the same considerations--especially related to sharing power--as discussed in **Models B-1** and **B-2**. We leave further discussion of logistics up to your imagination and creativity.

With co-writing, both authors own the copyrights; both names are on the cover; no author has more ownership than the other one. We recommend that both authors address why they are writing the story. It is not about a nmTC author writing the story of a mTC person, as often happens; both write, with horizontally-shared power. We recommend that authors have these agreements in writing and/or a pre-agreed-upon understanding of how they will resolve conflicts if they arise.

---------------------------- **MODEL B-4** ----------------------------

MODEL B-4: ADAPTATION OF PUBLISHED WORKS. Take an unsheltered, published text in the target language, and adapt it to simplified language for language-learners.

In the adaptation, include an authorization from the original author and, ideally, their community, stating that they approve of the adaptation's fidelity to the original publication. If the original author is not available, you might engage representatives of the original author's community. These representatives would not be simply people from the same region, or country, or with ties to the country, but rather, people with the characteristics of a sensitivity reader. Please see the section above on "Cultural Consultants and Sensitivity Readers.")

With an adaptation, if the content is "behind the curtain" (See Framework 6 ["Windows, Sliding-Glass Doors, Mirrors and Curtains"]) or reflects deep culture and high cultural-embeddedness (See Framework 4 ["Stories that 'Belong' to Others"), and if you are not a member of that culture, then you are almost certainly not the person to do the adaptation, <u>unless</u> members of that culture have specifically asked and authorized you to adapt the original publication for a language-learner audience.

The final product of an adaptation would ideally present both the unsheltered original publication and the sheltered version. The two versions could be presented perhaps side by side, or perhaps with one following the other (e.g. one version in the front of the book, and the other version in the back). If this is not feasible for the print copy of a book, consider including a link to a digital copy of the original. Inclusion of the original text maintains accountability so that members of the originating and receiving communities can see how you adapted the message from the original text.

Exceptions to showing the original text might occur with texts where the original publication is lengthy and is commonly available, such as *Don Quijote, 100 Years of Solitude*, etc.

You might consider adapting published works of fiction, non-fiction, poetry, etc., as well as newspaper and magazine articles. Keep in mind that you need permission from the original author and publisher before adapting any copyrighted works for public consumption. If a work is in the public domain (generally over 75 years old), such author/publisher permission is probably not needed.

In a preface or other supporting content in the adaptation, help readers understand the milieu in which the original work was written, for whom it was written and for what purpose. In other words, contextualize the text from historical, social, political, religious and other cultural perspectives.

We strongly recommend that your cultural consultants have a strong grounding in the original text and its original cultural context. You may want to invite the cultural consultant to write the above-referenced preface that contextualizes the text being adapted.

In an adaptation, although the goal is to adapt the language--not the story--due to the length of original publications as well as the needs of language learners, some abridging may be needed. Some considerations for abridging:
* You may want to survey members of the target culture to find out what parts of the material are most memorable and important to them.
* You may want to read literary analysis of classic texts--maybe even consulting with scholars working on the texts--in order to align your adaptation with the points that they see as most essential to the heart of the work.
* Ask your cultural consultants and sensitivity readers about the extent to which your abridging has captured the heart of the text. Work deeply with them to mitigate the effects of your own subconscious cultural lenses and priorities.

When doing abridging, explicitly state your cultural lenses, as storytelling styles differ across cultures, and readers benefit from knowing whose cultural cognitive frameworks are structuring the story. For more on this issue, refer to Framework 8 ("Cultural Styles of Storytelling").

Additional Notes on the Adaptation Model (B-4): We recommend attributing credit in the following manner: "Language and story simplified by [language-learner literature author from X cultural lenses] from the original text by [original author]."

With co-writing, both authors own the copyrights; both names are on the cover; no author has more ownership than the other one. We recommend that both authors address why they are writing the story. It is not about a nmTC author writing the story of a mTC person, as often happens; both write, with horizontally-shared power. We recommend that authors have these agreements in writing and/or a pre-agreed-upon understanding of how they will resolve conflicts if they arise.

---------------------------- **MODEL B-5** ----------------------------

MODEL B-5: CO-PRODUCTION OF A GRAPHIC NOVEL

Inspired by the collaboration between Omar Mohamed and Victoria Jamieson in the production of the young adult (YA) graphic novel *When Stars are Scattered*[84] (2020), we propose the development of graphic novels as a wide-open area for future collaborations between mTCs and nmTCs.

In *When Stars are Scattered,* Mohamed originally sought a ghostwriter to write his growing-up experience for adults; then, he met Victoria Jamieson, who offered her gifts of adapting stories into sheltered language for children via graphic novel format. He decided to take her up on the offer, and together they produced the graphic novel with his words, and her adaptation and illustrations[85].

In the creation of a graphic novel, each person plays a very distinct and necessary role for the telling of a story; the mTC author writes the story, and the graphic novel artist portrays the story through frame-by-frame illustrations of the advancing narrative, under the very close guidance of the oral storyteller. It is a true collaboration, as both oral storyteller and graphic artist bring their strengths.

This is distinct from simply illustrating a story, because in the graphic novel genre, plot developments are communicated through the pictures themselves.

Additional Notes on Model B-5:

- This is currently a lesser-used model in the field of language-learner literature, and given the wide popularity of graphic novels for the development of literacy in general, we recommend its expansion for the world language education field. Some authors of language-learner literature, notably Craig Klein Dexemple, have ventured into graphic novel development. We strongly encourage further work in this genre.

- This is similar to **Co-Writing (Model B-3)** in the degree of extremely close collaboration between author and illustrator.

- In this model, both the storyteller and the graphic novelist have their names on the cover. Both the storyteller and the writer are present in every stage of the process.

- Ensure close collaboration at every stage to ensure fidelity of the nmTC graphic novelist's work to the images in the mTC author's vision. Photographs are very helpful for the mTC author to present a more objective representation of their subjective perception to the nmTC graphic novelist.

---

[84] Omar Mohamed and Victoria Jamieson, *When Stars are Scattered,* ill. Iman Geddy (New York: Dial, 2020).

[85] Omar Mohamed and Victoria Jamieson, "How When Stars are Scattered Came to Be" [interview], Nerdy Book Club, November 2019, https://nerdybookclub.wordpress.com/2019/11/21/how-when-stars-are-scattered-by-victoria-jamieson-and-omar-mohamed-came-to-be/ (accessed 16 June 2020).

- Hire a colorist from the target culture, if possible, to do the colorization of the graphic novel illustrations. This requires financial output, of course, and it is worth it to ensure authentic representation.

Closing Reminder for Path B

For all the Path B models involving collaboration on the actual text—**B-2, B-3, B-4, B-5**--remember this point made in the discussion of **Model B-4:** With co-writing, both authors own the copyrights; both names are on the cover; no author has more ownership than the other one. We recommend that both authors address why they are writing the story. It is not about a nmTC author writing the story of a mTC person, as often happens; both write, with horizontally-shared power. Again, we recommend that authors have these agreements in writing and/or a pre-agreed-upon understanding of how they will resolve conflicts if they arise.

PATH C: FACILITATING

OVERVIEW: Path C leads to the production of works about target cultures. It is for authors who are not members of target cultures who seek to use their skill sets as consultants with new authors from target cultures, and/or to serve behind the scenes as a ghostwriter.

Note: If you desire to see your name on the cover of a book, then Path C is <u>not</u> the path for you.

------------------------ MODEL C-1 ------------------------

MODEL C-1: GHOSTWRITING

Ghostwriting is a process likely familiar to readers. It commonly occurs, for instance, when a famous person tells their autobiography and publishes it under their name, but it was actually written by a professional writer *other than* the famous person. This process could also occur, if carefully done, for the production of language-learner materials. Such ghostwritten materials might be an autobiography, a work of fiction or other genre of writing. This would be a strong choice for a storyteller who wants to tell a story but doesn't want to do the writing themselves; they might contract you to do the actual writing, and they--the storyteller--would serve as your guide along the way.

With ghostwriting, the issue of true and free consent prior to beginning a process leading to publication is essential. Just because someone appears to give consent does not indicate actual consent. Keep in mind that across lines of power, many opportunities exist for people to feel coerced. Ask yourself: Am I the best person to do this ghostwriting? Is there someone closer to the storyteller's culture that might be better positioned, in terms of cultural lenses, to ghostwrite this story?

If the storyteller is asking and authorizing *you* to write this story, by their own volition and consent--perhaps due to a personal relationship of trust that makes you their preferred ghostwriter--then consider these points as you proceed:

* Your ghostwriting is a collaborative effort; you will likely run many drafts past the original storyteller in order to have their full approval on your writing.

  * Be very cognizant of the filters of your paradigm. You will automatically process concepts and language through your own culturally-conditioned lenses which will almost certainly be different from those of the teller.[86] Your subjective lenses make the work not really the voice of the other person, no matter how hard you try. This is why you must have constant, consistent input from the teller to represent their phrasing and worldview to the maximum extent possible. Even so, you cannot fully step out of your own lenses. That is why we recommend the authorial credit as follows.

Authorial credit in Ghostwriting:
  - Credit in Ghostwriting goes <u>to the mTC storyteller.</u>
  - The nmTC ghostwriter's name is NOT stated. This anonymity of the ghostwriter helps to preserve the integrity of the process. It protects against the potential for the ghostwriter, whether consciously or subconsciously, to exploit the storyteller or the story for personal gain.
  - Although the ghostwriter's name is not stated, <u>do</u> state the nmTC ghostwriter's cultural identity so the reader knows what kind of cultural storytelling lenses were used. (For more on storytelling lenses, see Framework 8 ["Cultural Styles of Storytelling"] as well as the discussion in **Model B-4 (Adaptation)**.)
  - If the storyteller wishes to use a pseudonym, let the reader know nonetheless that a mTC has been the storyteller, stating the mTC's specific target culture and other relevant identity markers.

---

[86] "We make sense of perceptions and experiences through our particular cultural lens. This lens is neither universal nor objective…" Robin diAngelo, *White Fragility: Why it's so hard for White people to talk about racism* (Boston: Beacon, 2018), 9.

------------------------ **MODEL C-2** ------------------------

MODEL C-2: RECRUIT A NEW AUTHOR AND SERVE AS A CONSULTANT
In this model, you serve to recruit new authors and serve as consultant to a new author.

Recruiting: You pitch to mTCs in your network the need for sheltered-language stories for language learners. The mTC author chooses when, how and whether to write their story (which may extend beyond the individual level to include the story of their community or their ancestors).

Consulting: If the mTC author does not have familiarity with sheltering language for learners, then you could help make connections between the new author and the language-acquisition community of teachers and learner, <u>to the extent that the mTC author wants</u>. You would provide insider knowledge about the target audience of language-learners and language-teachers.

You might offer these skill sets and procedural knowledge bases:
- lists of core verbs (Super 7, Sweet 16, frequency dictionary)
- lists of cognates, if the target language / mTC author does not have a high knowledge of cognates between the target language and English
- benchmark examples of proficiency levels: what is a novice-mid, novice-high, intermediate-low, etc. book so the mTC author can tailor their work to that audience of language learner[87]
- criteria of what teachers' and districts' criteria with regard to equity issues[88]

Additional Notes on Model C-2:

- To reiterate: You are a resource behind the scenes, a process/skills consultant. Your name will probably not go on the book. The author might include your name in a "thanks" section if they want. There may or may not be financial compensation for you, depending on what you and the mTC author decide.
- Guard against any "White savior" mentality. You are not "saving" a new writer from obscurity. That quickly turns co-dependent and problematic. Instead, you are passing on your skills to a new writer, to the extent that they desire. Find a way, together, to make this a relationship of mutuality in which you both are giving and receiving.

---

[87] This is really important, given the dearth of materials for novices that are #OwnVoices and written by native speakers. Many materials intended to be "easy" are still too hard for novices.

[88] See, for example, "Guidelines for Positive Non-Stereotyped Portrayal of Human Roles in Curriculum Materials" from Des Moines School District (DMSD) in Iowa. DMSD uses these guidelines across subject areas. http://www.dmschools.org/wp-content/uploads/2011/10/AP-Biology-.pdf (accessed 28 June 2020).

- Be cognizant of internalized oppression: The mTC author may tell you 'Yes' due to socialization into a notion that "Europeans and North Americans know best." Meanwhile, you may unconsciously fulfill your part in this narrative of supremacy, despite your best intentions. Develop a working culture of critical reflection and shared, horizontal power.[89]
- While this consultant role may be filled by an nmTC teacher who has experience in yielding power to others, a bilingual native-speaker author (member of the same or different TC as the new author) may be the ideal consultant due to some increased likelihood of a more horizontal power structure. In this case, the nmTC teacher still would have a role to play in recruiting and in directing potential new authors to the native-speaker consultant.

---

[89] The emerging concept of "holocracy" in organizational leadership is helpful for horizontal power.

PATH D: SCRIBING

> OVERVIEW: Path D is ideal for language teachers who are not members of target cultures, and who may not (yet) consider themselves authors, and want to serve behind the scenes to accompany storytellers from target cultures in the creation of the storyteller's #OwnVoices texts.
>
> In Path D, the storyteller decides whether or not to later make their work appropriate for language-learners via Path B or C.
>
> If you implement Path D, please see Sensitivity Guidelines in Appendix I, especially with regard to issues of consent.

Scribing: Connect an oral or handwritten storyteller with <u>their</u> desired readership, using a model known in the world of literacy development as the **Language Experience Approach** or **"dictated stories."** This is not "X's story as told to Empire-identified author"; <u>this is the storyteller's own words</u>.

The Language Experience Approach is a staple of many early literacy programs for both first languages and additional languages[90], adapted here for the creation of language-learner literature. For simplicity, we refer to the Language Experience Approach / Dictated Stories simply as **"Scribing."**

---

[90] See Joan Wink, *The Power of Story* (Santa Barbara, CA: ABC-CLIO, 2018), 62-66; Denise D. Nessel and Carol L. Dixon, Ed. "Introduction to the Language Experience Approach," in *Using the Language Experience Approach with English Language Learners* (Thousand Oaks, CA: Corwin, 2008), 1-4. https://www.sagepub.com/sites/default/files/upm-binaries/21108_Introduction_from_Nessel.pdf (accessed 24 June 2020).

Who is involved in Scribing?
Storytellers: Scribing involves storytellers from target cultures who have a story to tell in the target language and prefer for someone else to write it down. It also may involve storytellers who want to author a handwritten manuscript and prefer for someone else to transfer it to typewritten form.
Scribes: This path, obviously, involves scribes. The scribe role is especially appropriate for language teachers who may not yet have skill sets as authors yet want to participate in bringing forth new stories into the publishing world.

Where might Scribing happen? The storytellers might connect with you in a local or an international context. They could be heritage speakers in your school; children; your neighbors; senior citizens; or anyone anywhere who has a story in the target language and feels that the physical act of writing, typing and/or reading is a barrier to telling that story.

How does Scribing work? In this path, the storyteller speaks; the scribe records in writing, verbatim, the storyteller's spoken words. The storyteller then reads or listens to[91] the text of what they have dictated, revising and expanding on ideas. The storyteller is the one who crafts any revision or expansion, not the scribe.

The scribe may then function in the additional role of beta audience, if the storyteller wishes, asking clarifying questions about content. At this point, the concern is *not yet* for the creation of comprehensible language-learner content. The final product at this stage is termed the "original version," produced in unsheltered language.

Alternate Process: The storyteller might write their story on paper, and then the scribe transfers it to digital print. This may be particularly appropriate if the storyteller does not have access to training in word processing skills.

The scribe makes clear from the beginning a commitment to confidentiality and to verbatim transcription, as well as the end goal: a final product that is created and owned entirely by the storyteller.

Who initiates Scribing? The scribe can make him/herself available, and storytellers can approach the scribe based on their own initiative.

What kinds of literature could be produced through Scribing? Any genre the storyteller wants to have scribed. The key here is that the storyteller decides what, when, how and how much to tell in the writing process with this particular scribe.

---

[91] Listening to the text can be a preferred option by many storytellers, including those who are culturally oriented to oral literacy over print literacy. If the storyteller is not the one reading aloud the text after the scribing, it might be ideal for a person from the storyteller's (sub)culture, of their choosing, to do the reading aloud, so that the storyteller is hearing the words reflected back in a voice that is possibly more similar to his/her/their own than the scribe's voice.

How is Scribing different from Ghostwriting (C-1)? With Scribing, the storyteller is producing a story *verbatim,* a story that can later be simplified for language learners by either the storyteller or someone the storyteller chooses. With Ghostwriting, the simplification typically takes place from the start.

Who is the audience for Scribing? The storyteller. The storyteller is the sole audience and possessor of the work they have asked you to scribe. Any further distribution--including any future simplification for language-learners--occurs at the initiative of the storyteller. You, as scribe, function in a confidential role.

* * *

Scribing is a unique form of accompaniment. An analogy to childbirth is fitting in describing Scribing. The storyteller is like a person giving birth to a baby: a book (or other genre of writing). The scribe provides the concrete, mechanical skill set to help to deliver that "baby"--like a midwife. The scribe also provides literary accompaniment--like a doula. Similar to a child-birthing doula, a literary doula may offer grounded emotional presence via attunement; reflective practices; bearing witness to the process; and encouragement. A literary doula may also offer engagement with the text as a beta reader, asking clarifying questions about parts that may seem unclear.

* * *

If your intention is to author and see your name on a book, then please do not engage in Scribing. That would harm the storyteller as this would be stealing their story. In this path, your name will be nowhere on the front of the book, as it is not your words. It goes without saying that you would not expect to receive financial compensation for this.

Who benefits from Scribing, and how? In Scribing, **the storyteller is the principal beneficiary** from the experience of producing a book over which s/he has total authorship and ownership.

In a mutual relationship, it is important that both sides know that the other is also benefiting from the experience. **Here are some ways that you as scribe may benefit from participating in Scribing:**

1) Potential contribution to language-learner literature: You may ultimately be helping to bring a new story to language learners (if that is the desire of the storyteller) via later simplification with **Model B-4 (Adaptation)** or **Model C-2 (Consult).**

2) Intangible personal benefits: You have the honor of assisting people in giving birth to their own story. You offer literary accompaniment and bear witness as the storyteller delves into expressing their imagination and inner worlds. You may hear feedback like "I've never written a story before but I now see myself as an author," "I can't wait to write more," or "Now that I've written this story, I feel I can close that chapter and move forward." You may forge a strong personal relationship with the storyteller.

3) **Extrinsic benefits:** This process is beneficial for the professional development of literacy specialists and language teachers. For literacy specialists: If the storyteller is a student in the process of acquiring reading skills, this is a powerful approach to literacy development. You will almost certainly observe increases in reading fluency and intrinsic motivation as the reader engages with their own story on the screen. Your modeling of writing processes may empower the storyteller to continue these processes independently in the future. For language teachers: This process may boost your own target-language speaking and listening proficiency, since you are listening to comprehensible, compelling input, and the speaker is confirming whether you accurately captured their dictation.

An important note about your own language proficiency: Assuming you are a certificated language teacher, your listening level is already likely at least at Advanced-Low. However, read the sensitivity notes in Appendix I about collaborating with a local native-speaker teacher if you are not at native-like proficiency with strong knowledge of regional language variations.

Essential Point: If you do Path D (Scribing), the story is in the hands of the storyteller. They decide what to do with it. You cannot get attached to any predetermined outcome such as this story making it to a language-learner audience. The storyteller may decide to keep the text for themselves and not share it. Or they may wish to share it with the world. It is their choice.

* * *

The storyteller has produced the text via Scribing… now what?

Creation of Simplified Language-Learner Version
Once the storyteller has completed the story, the storyteller may or may not choose to simplify the work for language learners. The simplification could happen in two ways:

> * **Option 1:** The storyteller creates the simplified content themselves, using the process described in **Model C-2 (Recruit a New Author / Serve as a Consultant)**. The scribe may transcribe the storyteller's simplifications. This route is theoretically preferable to Option 2 for putting the ownership in the storyteller's hands. Credit in Option 1: The credit goes to the storyteller. The scribe is behind the scenes. The storyteller may thank the scribe in the author's notes if the storyteller wishes, but this is not required. If the storyteller wishes to remain anonymous, please acknowledge nonetheless that an mTC is the author.

> * **Option 2:** The storyteller selects someone to create a simplified adaptation of the writing for language learners, (**Model B-4 Adaptation, with a crediting process similar to C-1 Ghostwriting**), under the direction of the storyteller and with their approval at each stage of the process, in a context of horizontal

leadership. The adaptor will need to ensure that the storyteller understands the goals and limitations of sheltered vocabulary, and to open up a continuous feedback loop so the storyteller can say, "Yes, you captured my intent," or "That misrepresents my story." <u>Credit in Option 2</u>: The original, unsimplified version is listed with the storyteller's name as author. The simplified version is also credited to the storyteller, with the acknowledgement of an *anonymous* adaptor. The adaptor does not get named on the book, although their cultural identity is stated in order to acknowledge different cultural storytelling styles (See Framework 8 ["Cultural Styles of Storytelling"]). This anonymity directs recognition and any and all profits to the storyteller and helps to protect their ownership over their story. It safeguards against the potential exploitation of the storyteller for the personal gain of the adaptor. If the storyteller wishes to remain anonymous, please acknowledge nonetheless that an mTC is the author.

The original version should accompany the simplified version in the published version of the book, perhaps in a back-to-back style (such as the style that the publisher *Fluency Matters* often uses to include two different language levels in one single book) or by dividing the text on each page spread (such as the full version on top and the adapted version on the bottom). Including the original version ensures that the storyteller's authentic voice remains available to the reader.

If the storyteller is a minor, you generally need parent/guardian consent to work with them in this scribe capacity. If a minor storyteller wishes to collaborate with you or others to simplify their work for a language-learner audience, you need parent/guardian permission for public publishing. Ensure that the storyteller wishes to do the publishing and is under no pressure from adults in their lives. If they are sharing sensitive content, use pseudonyms for privacy. Even if they are sharing non-sensitive content, ensure that no locational information is published, and be aware that publishing online may open up a nascent writer to destructive criticism. Seek professional counsel about how to advise a storyteller under legal age who wishes to publish their work for the public.

Consent: With storytellers of all ages, the issue of consent prior to a process leading to publication is essential. Just because someone appears to give verbal consent does not indicate actual consent. See **sensitivity notes for Scribing** in **Appendix I**.

QUESTIONS AND ANSWERS

Q: Is it ok to write Path A (authoring stories from your own [sub]cultures) in the "travel log" genre?

A: <u>Short Answer</u>: We recommend Path B (Collaboration) instead. <u>Long Answer</u>: In writing from your own perspective, you may desire to write about your experiences in another country as part of the "travel log" genre, as a personal diary written from your perspective as the traveller. We urge caution on this genre. You are the outside observer to that country, and you are only able to process your observations through the cognitive categories available to you from within your own cultural subjectivity. Hence, unfortunately, you will almost always unintentionally misrepresent what you see when you describe your observations as a traveler. The exception here might be for someone with sustained, strong connections with another country, writing with cultural consultants and sensitivity readers about surface cultural topics. (See FAQ below, "What if I have a strong connection to a target country?") In writing in the "travel log" genre, then, we recommend a collaborative model from **Path B** as part of the principle of "staying in our lanes."

Q: Why do we stress "staying in our lanes" so fervently?

A: We have seen repeatedly that when authors write stories that do not belong to them, many issues of misrepresentation and harm occur. Often the author and audience don't even realize it, which perpetuates the problem. It's not just a White problem, either; often, even teachers of color may not recognize the misrepresentation, and then proceed to give their approval (which may consist of something as nebulous as a "like" on Facebook), which others, particularly White people, proceed to interpret as a blanket statement of approval on the book--its content, process and problematic aspects--as if a statement of approval by a single person of color could somehow represent the approval of all the members of the particular target culture misrepresented in the book.[92]

For a thorough listing of issues of misrepresentation and harm that may occur, please revisit Framework 4 ("Stories that 'Belong' to Others + The Problems We Perpetuate").

---

[92] White supremacist ideas have been so embedded in Empire-identified cultures and internalized by historically-oppressed communities that they sometimes get perpetuated and approved of by Black, Indigenous, People of Color.

Q: What if I have strong connections with a target culture?
A: If you have sustained engagement with a target culture, then you might write about your experiences in that culture, taking caution with regard to the issues mentioned above in the discussion of the "travel log genre." Write in tandem with cultural consultants and sensitivity readers. (If you love a culture, don't present its deep stories; that is exploitation. Prove your love and relationship in the stories you write.) Also, consider using the financial proceeds to benefit the community. For suggestions on authoring with caution, see the traffic light metaphor in the next section.

Q: If I write from my own cultural perspective, doesn't that leave unfulfilled my professional expectations to teach about target cultures?
A: Clearly, not every language-learner book has to "teach target cultures" or be set in a target culture. Also, interculturality does require that we know ourselves. However, we do have the professional obligation to teach about target cultures. To meet these expectations, we recommend using an #OwnVoices book from the target culture for a class novel. These novels generally need teacher guidance to walk students through the cultural layers so they can appreciate and understand the products, practices and perspectives of the target culture and love what they're reading. Also, if you are using a paired set of books as in **Model B-1**, a single book with alternating cultural voices as in **Model B-2**, or a co-written text with intermingling cultural voices as in **Model B-3**, the students will benefit from additional teacher guidance in the instructional objectives of deep-level comparisons of cultures.

Q: What about already-published works? What steps might exist for revision?
A: In response to this frequent question, we need to say that our project refrains from commenting on any specific work except to uplift books that might exemplify the models. However, speaking generally, we suggest some possible steps for consideration: revise and reprint existing print and digital books, or remove them entirely from sale; issue public statements addressing problematic aspects of specific works; issue printable memoranda to insert in printed books about desired revisions (and perhaps invite readers who are mTCs to take up the challenge of rewriting the plotline from their particular cultural perspective). There are probably many more possibilities. Undoubtedly these kinds of revisions will become more efficient as the digitization of creative works empowers real-time updates. We applaud the creators of printed, digital and video content who are currently acknowledging and making amends for work that has had a harmful impact. Further discussion of how authors might amend past works lies beyond the scope of this book, and we hope these thoughts stimulate continued reflection on new possibilities.

Q: Could the Staying in Our Lanes team recommend specific people as sensitivity readers and as cultural consultants?

A: We hesitate to recommend specific people for these two roles for a variety of reasons, one of which is that the kind of persons who will be a good fit for one or the other of these roles will vary from book to book. We can recommend, however, that you contact the relevant departments at your local university, as they may have graduate students with very keen eyes for critical reading who would welcome the chance to add this kind of work to their resume for a relatively low cost. You may also want to hire a freelance sensitivity reader or cultural consultant from a service like Fiverr.

SUMMARY: "TRAFFIC LIGHT" METAPHOR

In summary, this "traffic light" graphic illustrates our recommendations for how non-members of particular target cultures might proceed in authoring stories: what would be off-limits (red); what might be done with caution (yellow); and what would be freely available as next avenues for increasing language-learner literature for students while honoring principles of the #OwnVoices movement (green).

Do not cross: Reserve these stories for authors from target cultures.
* higher-culturally-embedded stories that belong to cultures that are not your own, especially if they belong to colonized cultures (whether internationally-colonized or intranationally-colonized within the same country)

This includes stories of Indigenous cultures with whom you do not identify. Leave stories of Indigenous cultures for people who identify with those Indigenous nations either currently or ancestrally (as part of the reclamation of their roots, as described above in the definition of mTC).

See chart in Framework 4 ("Stories that 'Belong' to Others") for a list of characteristics of higher-culturally-embedded stories.

Proceed with caution: If you have a *strong connection to another culture* (as defined in the Defining Terms section above), you might very carefully consider authoring a story from a target culture across a cross-cultural line IF...

   * The story has a lower-cultural-embeddedness (see chart in Framework 4 ["Stories that 'Belong' to Others"]).
   * The story is invented (is not someone's actual story, and is not inspired by someone's actual story).
   * You collaborate with cultural consultants and sensitivity readers (see the elaboration on these roles at the beginning of the Paths).

Keep in mind that even lower-culturally-embedded, invented stories can be harmful if they essentialize, generalize, and perpetuate stereotypes. Cultural consultants and sensitivity readers are indispensable.

Proceed freely!
Path A: Author stories from your own (sub)cultures!
....
Proceed freely using the ethical considerations elaborated in this book:
Path B: Collaborate with a mTC author
Path C: Facilitate a new mTC author's work
Path D: Scribe an mTC storyteller's story

AN INVITATION TO CONTINUAL INNOVATION, TRANSPARENCY AND ACCOUNTABILITY

Innovation: The models described in this book under Paths A, B, C and D are ideas to get us started. There are possibly many more models to explore in these paths! Let's be in conversation about these models, as a profession, to discover additional models for meeting the goals of the 5 Cs of the ACTFL World-Readiness standards, producing simplified language-learner literature, and fostering respectful interculturality by honoring #OwnVoices from target cultures.

Transparency: In all the models proposed, we recommend the authors be transparent in the book's preface about the process involved. Readers want to know about ethics of not just the product but the process: the purpose, the accountability, and the vetting.

Accountability: As mentioned in the philosophical introduction, we are accountable not only to our students today, but our students ten years from now. Let's be ahead of the game with regard to what's happening in the academy with studies of colonization and critical theory, and how this plays out in the processes by which we generate materials, so that our materials can still be usable and highly regarded for a while into the future. More importantly, let's seek out and follow the strongest ethical practices possible, as teachers of language and interculturality, in order to dismantle historic and current systems of oppression and to support the liberation of all.

·····

POST-NOTE

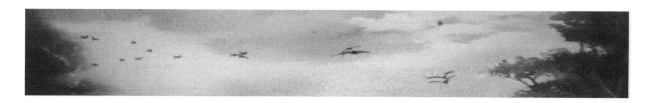

The final stage of the observe-analyze-act cycle of praxis is to begin observation again.

After implementing the models on these paths, we in our profession need to observe and reflect, gathering input from readers and communities. What can we celebrate? What needs improvement? The models will need to be analyzed, tweaked, expanded, re-thought, revised in an ever-repeating cycle of observe-analyze-act as our world of language-learner literature and broader cultural context evolves and grows. If it's 2025 and you are picking up this book that was created in 2020-2021, please look into what has transpired in the meantime!

This book has discussed transnational colonialism in our global context of world language education. For readers in North America, we strongly recommend following the leadership of Indigenous, Black, POC groups in the United States and Canada for understanding the calls for dismantling colonialism in local contexts.

Appendices, Works Cited, About the Authors

Appendix I: Essential Sensitivity Notes on Path D (Scribing)

These notes are birthed out of extensive reflection from one of our authors (Kristi) being a practitioner of this path. Please skip if Path D is not of interest.

Scribe's role as a guest: In any scribing situation, the scribe is a guest to the storyteller's inner and outer worlds. The scribe is not an expert but a servant of the storyteller.

Consent: As mentioned previously for other paths: With storytellers of all ages, the issue of consent prior to beginning a process leading to publication is essential. Just because someone appears to give consent does not indicate actual consent. Keep in mind that across lines of power, many opportunities exist for people to feel coerced.

Guarding against White saviorism: The Scribing process can be deeply rewarding for both the storyteller and scribe. However, keep in mind that you are not "saving" anyone in this process. In my (Kristi's) case of doing this process with teens in an cross-cultural context, my North American whiteness was not needed; local literacy teachers could have played the same role. The key aspect of my involvement was my free time as a volunteer to spend 8 hours a day doing 1:1 teen writer's workshops while local teachers were busy working in the classroom. Ideally, a local literacy teacher would be the person better suited for this role, or at minimum, a collaboration with local teachers so that the teens have sustainable access to a scribe from their local context.

The Delicate Art of Not Overcorrecting: In Scribing, you will be typing the person's story, and as you serve as scribe, you naturally take on the role of redactor (editor[93]) to align spoken speech with the typical grammatical structures of written text. For example, if you are doing Scribing in Spanish and the storyteller says *"O sea, yo tuve que ir..."* (roughly translated as "Um, I had to go...") you will probably omit *"O sea..."* ("Um..."). You probably won't announce this redaction; it would simply happen naturally as you type the storyteller's dictation with the assumption that the storyteller doesn't intend to include "filler" words in the writing.

You may also find yourself consciously or subconsciously "adjusting" the storyteller's spoken grammar to a standard written grammar. For example, if the storyteller dictates *"Quiero que vienes aquí,"* ("I want you to come here," with nonstandard grammar) you as a language teacher may want to type *"Quiero que vengas aquí"* (same meaning, with standard grammar), especially if you think that language learners may be reading this text someday. You will probably make a judgment call about whether to redact in the moment of typing, or whether to leave it as spoken and potentially discuss the choice later with the storyteller. In most situations, we recommend the latter, with very

---

[93] The word "redactor" appears instead of the more common English synonym "editor." In Spanish, "editor" has a secondary definition of "publisher," which could mislead some readers; "redactor" is a true cognate.

strong cautions about linguistic imperialism. Keep in mind, too, that your own understanding of target-language grammar may not be as well-developed as you may think!

We recommend that you and the storyteller discuss mutually any suggestions for grammar redactions. In this conversation, you as scribe function as a beta audience and might give feedback on what the storyteller's particular grammatical choice might communicate to the reader; together develop a few different options; and honor the storyteller's power to decide which grammatical option sounds most natural to their ears. Keep in mind the humility of your role: *the storyteller* is the expert on their own language; make clear that your intention is not to "correct" but to ensure congruence between the intended and received messages. If the storyteller has expressed a desire for language learners to read their work, then the needs of that audience could inform the conversation about grammar choices.

In general, it seems appropriate to redact grammar and punctuation to the level that a local, native-language copyeditor would. If the storyteller is a child or teen, consider what sorts of redactions a grammar teacher at their school might make. Ideally, consult with a local grammar teacher, for the risk is that as someone external to the region, you may "over-correct" language and unduly change the storyteller's voice, which is a form of linguistic imperialism. You may also transfer punctuation conventions from your first language into the target language, not realizing that different languages punctuate differently (e.g. Spanish and English use commas differently). Overcorrection, inappropriate correction, and inaccurate punctuation not only alter #OwnVoices, but they also may communicate to the storyteller the false and harmful notion that their language is somehow substandard or not acceptable in comparison with a Spanish speaker of Empire-identified identity--again, a form of linguistic imperialism.

Cultural Humility of Non-Native Speakers, and Ideal Situations: When you are fulfilling this redactor aspect of scribing and are not a native speaker, bear in mind that your role may create some cognitive dissonance for a storyteller: "How is it that this person doesn't fully speak my language yet can write more 'correctly' than me?" This sense may be lessened if the storyteller is a child and is accustomed to adults having more grammatical precision. Nonetheless, the ideal is for you to be "vetted" by a local native-language writer, or local native-language teacher, who can attest to the storyteller that your written language capacities are competent and explain that you are serving as a proxy for that writer/teacher, under their supervision.

Keep in mind, too, the regional particularities of language use. For this reason, as well as the ones discussed above, the ideal scribe/redactor would likely be a native-TL-speaker from the region of the storyteller. A native TL speaker from a different region might also be ideal for this role if they have knowledge of regional language variations.

Despite the proposal in this book of Path D as an avenue for nmTC teachers, the most ideal role of a non-native speaker of the TL may be as an advocate of the process who networks to recruit native speakers to serve as scribes.

Recognize, of course, that the above points are ideals. Depending on your skill on the "delicate art of not overcorrecting," the warm synergy and humility of your relationship with the storyteller, and the general availability of scribes in the storyteller's context, the ideal person may be you, as a highly proficient but not native speaker. Nevertheless, be willing to cede your role when a native speaker, especially a native speaker from the region, is interested, willing and able to take on the immensely joyous role of helping another to bring their stories to birth.

Appendix II: FAQs on the #OwnVoices Movement

Corinne Duyvis, author of young adult literature and originator of the #OwnVoices hashtag, has written a helpful piece on frequently asked questions about the #OwnVoices movement. It can be accessed online at http://www.corinneduyvis.net/ownvoices/. We offer here a summary. All quotations come from the above-mentioned webpage.

* The #OwnVoices hashtag originated in September 2015 on Twitter as a way to recommend children's and young adult literature "about diverse authors written by authors from that same diverse group."

* The #OwnVoices hashtag can be used for any marginalized identity, "as long as the protagonist and the author share a marginalized identity." The author and protagonist don't need to share every aspect of their identity, but rather, *an* aspect of identity. #OwnVoices means that the actual author shares this identity with the protagonist, not the author's family member, friend, student, etc.

* A shared marginalized identity needs to be somewhat particular, not broad. For instance, if the disability aspect of a protagonist's identity is intended to be #OwnVoices, the author and character should share that *specific* disability. For instance, using an example Duyvis provides, iif an Autistic author writes a Blind character, it would be inappropriate to say that the disability aspect of the novel is #OwnVoices.

* When describing works as #OwnVoices, it is helpful to name which aspect of the identity of a protagonist is #OwnVoices. Duyvis gives the example "Cool Heist Book features a Chinese-American trans girl — the trans aspect is #ownvoices!" as one that is accurate and does not mislead potential readers, whereas "Cool Heist Book features a Chinese-American trans girl! #ownvoices" would mislead readers to believe that both identities were #OwnVoices.

* Due to mutiple intersecting identities in protagonists and authors, even an #OwnVoices work can feature a protagonist with vastly different experiences from the author, even though they share at least one marginalized identity. For instance, as Duyvis describes, a Black and Deaf person will have a very different experience from someone who is White and Deaf, or someone who is Black and hearing. Duyvis acknowledges that this complicates what books can be considered #OwnVoices, but does not advocate that #OwnVoices should be restricted to books in which an author and protagonist share every identity, citing two main reasons: 1) it would be harder to produce and to find #OwnVoices literature; and 2) it would pressure marginalized authors to write characters who are like them in every major identity aspect.

* Just because a book has the #OwnVoices label does not mean it or its author is exempt from criticism. The #OwnVoices label is "not an automatic seal of approval, authenticity of quality." An author can still write "outside of their lane" while technically writing #OwnVoices.

* #OwnVoices "is *not* about policing or pressuring" marginalized authors to write about any particular topic or character."

* #OwnVoices describes a work, not an author. Sometimes an author might write an #OwnVoices work, and sometimes they might not.

* In response to a question about if "privileged authors shouldn't write marginalized protagonists," Duyvis responds that "People can write about whatever they want; whether they should is a valid and complex discussion…" Duyvis elaborates with a quote cited earlier in this book, in Framework 7 ("#OwnVoices"): "Historically speaking, it's extremely common for marginalized characters to be written by authors who aren't part of that marginalized group and who are clueless despite having good intentions. As a result, many portrayals are lacking at best and damaging at worst. Society tends to favor privileged voices even regarding a situation they have zero experience with, and thus those are the authors that get published."

* #OwnVoices is not about pressuring or putting obligation on any author "to disclose any part of their identity." Safety and privacy are valued, and the label involves aspects of identity that an author has chosen to make public. It goes without saying that if anyone has knowledge about an author's identity that the author has not made public, then the work should not be labeled "OwnVoices" without the author's explicit consent.

Appendix III: Recommended Resources and Movements

Websites

- Learning for Justice (formerlyTeaching Tolerance), Social Justice "Can-Do" Standards (learningforjustice.org/sites/default/files/2017-06/TT_Social_Justice_Standards_0.pdf)

- "Teaching for Intercultural Competence" Facebook Group (facebook.com/groups/TeachingforICC)

- "We Teach Languages" Podcast (weteachlang.com)

- Diversify Your Bookshelf (facebook.com/groups/diversifyyourbookshelf)

- We Need Diverse Books (diversebooks.org)

- Continental Maps at Native Land (native-land.ca) and Indigenous Peoples Resources (indigenouspeoplesresources.com)

- Krishauna Hines-Gaither, Cup of Diversity (cupofdiversity.com)

- Anna Gilcher and Rachelle Adams, Elevate Education Consulting (elevateeducationconsulting.com)

- Cécile Lainé, Toward Proficiency (towardproficiency.com)

- Language-Learner Literature Advisory Board (LLLAB) (wearelllab.org)

- Learning for Justice (formerly Teaching Tolerance), Reading Diversity guide (learningforjustice.org/magazine/publications/reading-diversity)

Hashtags

- #WeNeedDiverseBooks
- #WLBookAudit
- #DignidadLiteraria / #LiteraryDignity
- #DiversityJedi
- #DiversityGap
- #DisruptTexts

Recommended Authors on "the Decolonial Turn" and Postcoloniality

Nelson Maldonado-Torres, the Puerto Rican philosopher who developed the term *decolonial turn / el giro descolonial*, describes the "massive theoretical and epistemological breakthroughs in the works of Third World figures, such as, for instance, **Frantz Fanon, Enrique Dussel, Aníbal Quijano, and Sylvia Wynter**" as well as "a younger but not less illustrious generation of scholars, including **Linda Martin Alcoff, Lewis Gordon, María Lugones, Walter Mignolo, Chela Sandoval,** and **Catherine Walsh**, and in collectives such as the **modernity/coloniality/decoloniality network**, the **Caribbean Philosophical Association**, and in a varied group of Latina/o philosophers and critics."[94] We are grateful to Maldonado-Torres for this list of scholars and collectives to follow, and as he is coming principally from a Spanish-language perspective, a French-speaking colleague has suggested these additional scholars: **Aimé Césaire, Albert Memmi, Léopold Sédar Senghor, Françoise Vergès.** We would add to these lists: **Henri Giroux, Paulo Freire, Eduardo Galeano, Masood Raja, Homi Bhabha, Gayatri Chakravorty Spivak** (especially her seminal essay, "Can the subaltern speak?"), and **Edward Said**. It should be noted that all of these authors represent an array of views and that our recommendation of their work does not, of course, necessarily entail endorsement of every philosophy that any particular author proposes. Also, we should note that we have not yet read from all these authors but are on a journey. This list is a jumping-off point into the wide field of voices in decolonial/postcolonial studies from a global perspective.

The authors recommended above write from a variety of locations worldwide. We strongly recommend following leadership of local Indigenous, Black, POC groups for understanding the call for dismantling colonialism in one's local context.

---

[94] Maldonado-Torres, "Thinking through the decolonial turn," 5-6.

Works Cited

American Council on the Teaching of Foreign Languages, NCSSFL-ACTFL Can-Do Statements: Proficiency Benchmarks (2017), https://www.actfl.org/sites/default/files/CanDos/Intercultural%20Can-Do_Statements.pdf (Accessed 26 June 2020).

American Council on the Teaching of Foreign Languages, "World-Readiness Standards for Learning Languages" (2015), https://www.actfl.org/sites/default/files/publications/standards/World-ReadinessStandardsforLearningLanguages.pdf (Accessed 26 June 2020).

American Psychological Association, "Racial and Ethnic Identity," 2020, https://apastyle.apa.org/style-grammar-guidelines/bias-free-language/racial-ethnic-minorities (Accessed 22 October 2020).

Angelelli, Enrique. Quoted in "Hay Que Seguir Andando Nomás," UP Santa Fe [blog], https://unidadpopularsantafe.org/2016/08/01/hay-que-seguir-andando-nomas/ (Accessed 20 July 2020).

Associated Press, "Explaining AP Style on Black and White," 20 July 2020, https://apnews.com/article/9105661462

Calle 13 [band]. "Latinoamérica." Track 7 on *Entren los que quieran*. Sony Music, audio recording (4:58). Calle 13, performed with Totó la Momposina, Susana Baca, Maria Rita y Gustavo Santaolalla, 2010.

Campbell, Edith. "The Problem with Picture Book Monkeys: Racist imagery associating simians with Black people has a long history." *School Library Journal*. 4 December 2019. https://www.slj.com/The-Problem-with-picture-book-monkeys-racist-imagery-libraries (Accessed 9 July 2020).

Césaire, Aimé. *Discourse on Colonialism*. Translated by Joan Pinkham. New York: Monthly Review Press, 2000. Originally published as *Discours sur le colonialisme*. Editions Présence Africaine, 1955.

Chenoweth, Robin. "Rudine Sims Bishop: 'Mother of Multicultural Children's Literature'." Ohio State University, 5 September 2019. https://ehe.osu.edu/news/listing/rudine-sims-bishop-diverse-childrens-books/ (Accessed 10 June 2020).

Committee of Black Writers of the Writer's Guild of America West (WGAW). "Letter to Hollywood From WGAW Committee of Black Writers," 12 June 2020. https://www.wga.org/uploadedfiles/the-guild/inclusion-and-equity/dear_hollywood_june_12_2020.pdf

Conlon Perugini, Dorie. (Interviewer), Johnson, S.M. (Producer). (2020). We Teach Languages Episode 142: Language Legitimacy and Imagining New Educational

Contexts with Jonathan Rosa [Audio podcast], 33:13-13:54. https://weteachlang.com/2020/06/12/142-with-jonathan-rosa/ (Accessed 22 June 2020).

Crayton, Kim. "Stop Recommending #WhiteFragility as a #AntiRacist Resource" (video), 2:00-2:08. https://www.pscp.tv/w/1BdxYnjQklMKX (Accessed 24 June 2020).

Cromwell, Michelle. "Racism: The challenge of dismantling lies in the dilemma of definition." In *Encyclopedia of Diversity and Social Justice* (ed. Sherwood Thompson). Maryland: Rowman and Littlefield, 2015.

Cummins, Jeanine. *American Dirt.* London: Tinder Press, 2020.

Danziger, Paula, and Martin, Ann M. *P.S. Longer Letter Later.* New York: Scholastic, 1998.

Delpuech, André. "Colonisation and Slavery: For a Necessary and Rightful Place in Heritage and Museums." International Council of Museums, 19 January 2021. https://icom.museum/en/news/colonisation-and-slavery-archaeology/ (Accessed 7 March 2021).

Des Moines School District. "Guidelines for Positive Non-Stereotyped Portrayal of Human Roles in Curriculum Materials." Des Moines, Iowa. http://www.dmschools.org/wp-content/uploads/2011/10/AP-Biology-.pdf (Accessed 28 June 2020).

DiAngelo, Robin. *White Fragility: Why it's so hard for White people to talk about racism.* Boston: Beacon, 2018.

Dignidad Literaria. "*#DignidadLiteraria press conference.*" 2020. https://dignidadliteraria.com (Accessed 27 November 2020).

Doña Angela, "De Mi Rancho a Tu Cocina" (video channel). https://www.youtube.com/channel/UCJjyyWFwUIOfKhb35WgCqVg/videos (Accessed 26 June 2020).

Duyvis, Corinne. "#OwnVoices," *Corinne Duyvis: Sci-Fi and Fantasy in MG and YA* [blog]. Undated post. http://www.corinneduyvis.net/ownvoices/ (Accessed 3 July 2020).

Fakoly, Tiken Jah. "Plus rien ne m'étonne." Track 1 on *Coup de guele.* Barclay Records, 2004. https://g.co/kgs/RVZbhQ (Accessed 7 March 2021).

Gaab, Carol. *Brandon Brown Quiere un Perro [Brandon Brown Wants a Dog].* Denver, CO: Fluency Matters, 2013.

Galeano, Eduardo. *Open veins of Latin America: Five centuries of the pillage of a continent.* Translated by Cedric Belfrage. NYU Press, 1997. Originally published as *Las venas abiertas de América Latina.* Madrid: Siglo Veintiuno, 1971.

Greene-Moton, Ella, and Minkler, Meredith. "Cultural Competence or Cultural Humility? Moving Beyond the Debate." *SAGE Pub*, 12 November 2019. https://doi.org/10.1177/1524839919884912 (Accessed 28 November 2020).

Grosfoguel, Ramón. "The structure of knowledge in westernized universities: Epistemic racism/sexism and the four genocides/epistemicides." *Human Architecture: Journal of the sociology of self-knowledge* 1 (2013): 73-90. https://scholarworks.umb.edu/cgi/viewcontent.cgi?article=1445&context=humanarchitecture, (accessed 17 July 2020).

Hammond, Zaretta. *Culturally Responsive Teaching and The Brain: Promoting Authentic Engagement and Rigor Among Culturally and Linguistically Diverse Students*. Thousand Oaks, CA: Corwin, 2014.

Hines-Gaither, Krishauna. "Anti-Racism in the World Language Classroom." *WorldView: A Language Blog*, Concordia Language Villages, 14 July 2020. http://www.concordialanguagevillages.org/blog/villages/anti-racism-in-the-world-language-classroom#.Xw8PmC3Mw6V (Accessed 15 July 2020).

Jackson, Catrice M. "'Get In Your Lane Anti-Racism Workshop." *Catriceology,* ndated (copyright 2015-2020). http://www.catriceology.com/get-in-your-lane-workshop (Accessed 13 July 2020).

Jacobsen, Matthew Frye. *Whiteness of a Different Color: European Immigrants and the Alchemy of Race*. Cambridge, MA: Harvard, 1999.

James, Laura. *Odd Girl Out: My Extraordinary Autistic Life*. Berkeley, CA: Seal, 2018.

Kang, Kang. Interview with Françoise Vergès. "To Dismantle the Master's Tools: An Interview with Françoise Vergès." *South of the South* (Issue 1). Undated. Available online at https://www.timesmuseum.org/en/journal/south-of-the-south/an-interview-with-fran-oise-verg-s (Accessed 7 March 2021).

Kuo, Lily. "Instagram's White Savior Barbie neatly captures what's wrong with 'voluntourism' in Africa." Quartz Africa, 20 April 2016. https://qz.com/africa/665764/instagrams-white-savior-barbie-neatly-captures-whats-wrong-with-voluntourism-in-africa/ (Accessed 7 March 2021).

Lainé, Cécile. *Camille: Le Studio de Danse*. Self-published, 2019.

Maldonado-Torres, Nelson. "Thinking through the decolonial turn: Post-continental interventions in theory, philosophy, and critique—An introduction." *Transmodernity: Journal of Peripheral Cultural Production of the Luso-Hispanic World* 1.2 (2011), https://dialnet.unirioja.es/descarga/articulo/3979025.pdf (Accessed 27 November 2020).

Mohamed, Omar, and Jamieson, Victoria. *When Stars are Scattered,* ill. Iman Geddy. New York: Dial, 2020.

Mohamed, Omar, and Jamieson, Victoria. "How When Stars are Scattered Came to Be" [interview]. *Nerdy Book Club*, November 2019. https://nerdybookclub.wordpress.com/2019/11/21/how-when-stars-are-scattered-by-victoria-jamieson-and-omar-mohamed-came-to-be/ (Accessed 16 June 2020).

Motha, Suhanthie. *Race, empire, and English language teaching: Creating responsible and ethical anti-racist practice.* New York: Teachers College Press, 2014.

National Museum of African American History and Culture. "Talking About Race: Whiteness." Undated. https://nmaahc.si.edu/learn/talking-about-race/topics/whiteness (Accessed 28 November 2020).

Nessel, Denise D. and Dixon, Carol L., Ed. "Introduction to the Language Experience Approach." In *Using the Language Experience Approach with English Language Learners* (Thousand Oaks, CA: Corwin, 2008), 1-4. https://www.sagepub.com/sites/default/files/upm-binaries/21108_Introduction_from_Nessel.pdf (Accessed 24 June 2020).

Ngozi Adichie, Chimamanda. "The Danger of a Single Story" (2009), TEDGlobal 2009, https://www.ted.com/talks/chimamanda_ngozi_adichie_the_danger_of_a_single_story/transcript (Accessed 15 June 2020).

Olsen, Laurie. *Made in America: Immigrant Students in Our Public Schools.* New York: The New Press, 2008.

Oxford Dictionary. "Locus." https://www.lexico.com/en/definition/locus (Accessed 28 November 2020).

Quintero, A.C. *La clase de confesiones: Carlos hace el peor error de su vida.* Self-published, 2017.

Raja, Masood. "Postcolonialism Course (Edited Version), Session 11: *Efuru*: Discussion and Q & A" [Video, 50:21]. Postcolonialism [YouTube Channel]. https://www.youtube.com/watch?v=OJkJO2FJvjU&list=PLW4ijepGeAnb60jNHo7jxcdBUwSocZUHO&index=18&fbclid=IwAR1Sgy6w-Qya2-uN1_tbuMRs57WwR3tn7iriiq4-F5yDAT8gQRycCgQQog (Accessed 9 February 2021).

Ramírez, Adriana. *Un nuevo amanecer,* illustrated by Santiago Aguirre. Self-published, 2020.

Ray, Blaine. *Pobre Ana: Una novela breve y fácil totalmente en español,* ed. Contee Seely. Berkeley, CA: Command Performance Language Institute, 2000.

Reese, Debbie. "Critical Indigenous Literacies: Selecting and Using Children's Books about Indigenous Peoples," *Language Arts* 95.6 (2018), 390-391.

Robison, Katie. "Final Thoughts: Stay in Your Lane." *Katie Robison* [blog]. 8 October 2017. https://katierobison.com/improving-representation-final-thoughts/ (Accessed 13 July 2020).

Rodriguez, Tanya. "Decolonization, A Guide for Settlers Living on Stolen Land." *Tanya Rodriguez* [blog], 26 December 2020. https://gdiriseup.medium.com/decolonization-a-guidebook-for-settlers-living-on-stolen-land-57d4e4c04bbb (Accessed 15 April 2021).

Ross, Loretta. "The origin of the term 'women of color'" [interview], Western States Center, 28 January 2011, https://www.youtube.com/watch?v=82vl34mi4Iw (Accessed 18 January 2021).

Schutte, Ofelia. "Philosophy, Postcoloniality, and Postmodernity." In *A Companion to Latin American Philosophy*. Eds. Susana Nuccetelli, Ofelia Schutte, and Otávio Bueno, 312-326. Malden, MA: Wiley-Blackwell, 2013.

Sims Bishop, Rudine. "Mirrors, Windows, and Sliding Glass Doors." *Perspectives: Choosing and Using Books for the Classroom* 6.3 (Summer 1990).

Spivak, Gayatri Chakravorty: "Can the Subaltern Speak?". In *Marxism and the Interpretation of Culture*. Eds. Cary Nelson and Lawrence Grossberg. Urbana, IL: University of Illinois Press, 1988: 271-313.

Táíwò, Olúfẹ́mi. "Don't Stand With Me." *Blog of the APA [American Psychological Association]*, 30 June 2020. https://blog.apaonline.org/20230/dont-stand-with-me/ (Accessed 13 July 2020).

Tuck, Eve, and K. Wayne Yang. "Decolonization is not a metaphor." *Decolonization: Indigeneity, Education & Society* (Vol. 1, No. 1, 2012). https://clas.osu.edu/sites/clas.osu.edu/files/Tuck%20and%20Yang%202012%20Decolonization%20is%20not%20a%20metaphor.pdf (Accessed 25 March 2021).

United Nations Educational, Scientific and Cultural Organization (UNESCO). "Interculturality." https://en.unesco.org/creativity/interculturality (Accessed September 15, 2020)

Untitled Latinx Project. "Open Letter to Hollywood," October 2020. https://untitledlatinxproject.com/la-letter (Accessed 28 November 2020).

Washuta, Elissa. "Apocalypse Logic." The Offing, 21 November 2016. https://theoffingmag.com/insight/apocalypse-logic/ (Accessed October 22, 2020).

Wink, Joan. *The Power of Story*. Santa Barbara, CA: ABC-CLIO, 2018.

Writers Guild of America West (WGAW) Native American and Indigenous Writers' Committee (NAIWC). "Open Letter to Hollywood," 16 October 2020. https://www.wga.org/news-events/news/connect/10-16-20/native-american-indigenous-writers-committee-releases-open-letter-to-hollywood (Accessed 28 November 2020).

Woods, Ashton P. "Hey White People, Stay in Your Lane!" *#TheBlog,* 23 April 2017. https://www.ashtonpwoods.com/theblog/hey-White-people-stay-in-your-lane (Accessed 13 July 2020).

Young McChesney, Kay. "Teaching Diversity: The Science You Need to Know to Explain Why Race Is Not Biological." SAGE Open, 16 October 2015. https://journals.sagepub.com/doi/10.1177/2158244015611712 (Accessed 28 November 2020).

Zinn, Howard, with Stefoff, Rebecca. *A Young People's History of the United States: Columbus to the War on Terror.* New York: Penguin Random House, 2001.

ABOUT THE AUTHORS

We all three have intellectually authored this book through sustained conversations over many months, in synergy with broader conversations in the fields of language learning, literature, anti-racism and decolonization. The responsibility for word-crafting this book lies with Kristi, with deep collaboration from Adriana and Cécile. We thank another Cécile--Dr. Cécile Accilien--for her critical reading and insights for the manuscript, and for writing the foreword to the book in collaboration with Dr. Krishauna Hines-Gaither. We also deeply thank the beta readers and webinar participants whose insights have influenced this work, as well as our professional networks and cohorts of world language teachers. Your friendships and conversations have been deeply formative in this work. It is a joy to think and write in community.

Principal Writer: Kristi Lentz (she/her) is a world language teacher in Spanish/ESL and a reading/literacy specialist. She has taught with comprehensible input since 2010 and language-learner novels since 2016, and has been facilitating story production using Path D (Scribing/Language Experience Approach) throughout her career. Motivated by a drive to deepen curricular engagement toward peace and justice, she is currently working on a graduate degree concentrated on intercultural studies. She writes non-fiction and looks forward to co-authoring a Path B book. Kristi's roots are from German coal miners, Norwegian potato farmers and Minnesotan mail carriers; she hails from a predominantly White, suburban-rural region of Western Washington; she feels deeply formed by intercultural engagement in South, Central and North America over the last 25 years; and after four years living in the San Francisco Bay Area, she currently resides in rural Mendocino County, California. She values these personal roots as well as her professional roots in WAFLT, ACTFL, iFLT and online world language communities dedicated to continuous reflection, growth and collaboration. She is deeply committed to engaging with her own White people to collectively do the work of uncolonizing the "practices, products and perspectives" of White cultures (to use the terminology of the ACTFL World-Readiness Standards!)--an ongoing project of listening, relearning, and responding. Find her online at @lentzkristi (Twitter).

Collaborative Writers:
Adriana Ramírez (she/her/ella) is a Spanish teacher, author and teacher trainer. She teaches all levels of Spanish, from beginners to IB students, using comprehensible input methodologies. She is constantly coaching other teachers and presenting workshops in Canada, the US and Europe. She also holds a double major in Psychology, a degree in Clinical Psychology and a Master's degree in Education. She has a big passion for sharing with the world the beauty of her country and her people, and you can see this love through all her published novels. A big advocate of the #OwnVoices movement, Adriana strongly believes that those who come from traditionally oppressed and colonized countries and territories, must reclaim their right to tell their own stories and build their own narratives. This belief led her to be part of this project, as a way to help White authors

stay in their lanes, and stop reproducing the colonizer mentality with the stories they tell. Originally from Colombia, Adriana has Black, Indigenous and European roots. She actively works on recuperating the stories and the narrative that were erased by the colonizers, and that are part of her roots and her heritage. You can find her at @veganadri (Twitter and Instagram), adrianaramirez.ca, and her YouTube channel: 'Teaching Spanish with Comprehensible Input.'

Cécile Lainé (she/her) is a French teacher, coach, mentor, and author who has lived in France, England, Costa Rica, Poland, and the United States. Her second passion after being in the classroom with students is helping teachers to build joyful, inclusive, and acquisition-driven language classrooms. In 2016, she started Le Petit Journal Francophone, a monthly publication that brings a variety of compelling news stories from the Francophone world. In 2017, she created Diversify Your Bookshelf, a Facebook group for parents, educators, and librarians who want to bring a variety of books to their homes, classrooms, and libraries. In 2018, she worked at an all-girls school, and upon reviewing the language-learner literature available, she realized there were none with strong female characters. She has been attempting to fill this gap ever since by publishing language-learner readers featuring and empowering all girls (Path A). She is now continuing her journey by supporting teachers who wish to diversify their bookshelves, and authors who want to write #ownvoice books (Path C). The 'Staying in Our Lanes' project has also opened doors for her to write in Path B, which she is looking forward to. You can find her online at towardproficiency.com.

Made in the USA
Middletown, DE
26 November 2022